THE GOD WHO BECKONS

THEOLOGY IN THE FORM OF SERMONS

ROBERT CUMMINGS NEVILLE

DRAWINGS BY BETH NEVILLE

Abingdon Press
Nashville

THE GOD WHO BECKONS
THEOLOGY IN THE FORM OF SERMONS

Copyright © 1999 by Abingdon Press

This book is printed on acid-free paper.

Library of Congress Cataloging in Publication Data

Neville, Robert C.
  The God who beckons : theology in the form of sermons/ Robert Cummings Neville.
    p.   cm.
  ISBN 0-687-08481-4 (pbk. : alk. paper)
  1. Occasional sermons.   2. Sermons, American.   3. Methodist Church—Sermons.
I. Title.
BV4254.2.N48   1999
252'.076—dc21   98-48117
                                                                                CIP

The biblical quotations, unless noted otherwise, are from the New Revised Standard Version, copyrighted in 1989 by the Division of Christian Education of the National Council of the Churches of Christ in the United States of America.

Biblical citations marked NEB are from *The New English Bible.* © The Delegates of the Oxford University Press and The Syndics of the Cambridge University Press 1961, 1970. Reprinted by permission.

Citations of hymns are to *The United Methodist Hymnal* (Nashville: The United Methodist Publishing House, 1989).

99 00 01 02 03 04 05 06 07 08—10 9 8 7 6 5 4 3 2

MANUFACTURED IN THE UNITED STATES OF AMERICA

To the Faculty, Staff, and Students
of the Boston University School of Theology

Contents

PART FIVE: CHRISTIAN INTELLIGENCE

PREFACE

Holy fire, deep water, bleak abyss, and light are traditional Christian symbols, but wild ones, tending to exaggeration. They are not tame like the symbols arising from stories. Their very abstractness generalizes us beyond our circumstances to a more nearly God's-eye view of things. They consume, dissolve, empty, and penetrate boundaries. They are wild like Jesus. Each symbolizes a medium between our finite lives and the infinite. We pass through them to God, and light is the one that seems the last step. Most Christians have touched these symbols in song, prayer, and worship. They are not prominent in Scripture or doctrine, although some creeds call Christ "Light of light." Yet they are found in Scripture, often as the background symbols within which the action takes place; and their meanings are multiple and sometimes contradictory. These and symbols like them interpret our ordinary lives but also shake us free from more defined symbols to an awareness of the immensity of God.

The sermons here are mostly for special occasions with ordinary topics, and yet these symbols have made me look at the ordinary in a weird way so that it looks holy, like the Creator. In one way or another, then, these sermons are all about God, no matter what they say they are about. They are about God beckoning us through fire, water, and the abyss, into the divine light where we do not so much see God as dissolve in blissful love. If I were not a seminary dean, I'd think I was a mystic. The humbler truth is that I am a church bureaucrat who has lucked on to something Christianity offers everyone, and preach that.

These are sermons of a dean of a theological school whose field is theology and whose training was in philosophy. An unlikely preacher, you might say, combining a church bureaucrat's illusions of importance with an academic's irrelevance. You might be right, although I prefer another set of descriptions. I came to the deanship at the Boston University School of Theology in an academic career in which I had been a chairman or dean continuously since 1966. For this reason I view myself as more of a practical person than either spiritual or theoretical. As a philosopher and theologian I have had a journeyman's career, publishing scholary books and articles and taking part in professional organizations so that now I have something to say. It might not be profound, but it has developed out of an enduring engagement with the great issues of our generation. (For a plain, non-sermonic introduction to Christian doctrine, see my *A Theology Primer*; for religion in a scientific age, see *Eternity and Time's Flow*; for philosophical theology, see *God the Creator*, all SUNY Press.) As a spiritual person, I have been ordained a long time (deacon in 1963, elder in 1966, in the Methodist Church), fought the usual battles of the soul, served thirteen years as an associate pastor in the Bronx and another ten as a sometime associate in Long Island, before coming to Boston University. There is nothing outstanding in my spiritual life, except to me: I am overwhelmed by God's loveliness, despite all else. It's the conjunction of the practical, theological, and spiritual life that makes these sermons interesting, if they are; for it's in preaching that the dimensions of life come together.

Christian sermons ought first and foremost to present the good news of the gospel. In each of the sermons here, I have stepped back from the texts and from the occasion to ask, What is the gospel in this context, and how can it be expressed? Nearly every one of the sermons issues an invitation to join or invest more deeply in the Christian movement. But every biblical text requires interpretation, and so does every situation. Each congregation is different, and so is each occasion. All this requires interpretation both within a sermon and in the preparation of a sermon.

Although all Christian preachers work with biblical texts and attend to their audiences, they differ among themselves in the orientation and background they bring to their interpretations. Some are pastors, preaching week in and week out to the same congregation, ministering to its mission. Others are traveling church leaders—bishops, superintendents of various sorts, representatives of national boards, missionaries, evangelists—with specific portfolios in the background. Some view ministry psychologically as pastoral care, others as social action, or community enhancement, or spiritual formation; and we preach out of the interpretations shaped by those orientations. I preach as a theologian, an academic, and a theological educator.

Whereas preachers suffer chronic laryngitis, theologians suffer chronic neck pain caused by looking over their shoulders at other theologians. Neck pain is an appropriate occupational hazard because we theologians are responsible to one another for the imagination, daring, faithfulness, care, precision, sensitivity, and truth of our arguments. Without confidence in the scrutiny of other professionals, theologians tend to veer between excess timidity and wild irresponsibility. Timidity does no one any good, however much it might reinforce the self-righteousness of those who think they have everything figured out. Wild irresponsibility is popular and sells books but only makes some people feel good without changing the serious ways they think and live religiously. True theology engages both the varied conditions of daily life and the challenges of rapidly changing modern civilization, and addresses these with the religious resources of the tradition, beginning with the Bible and including what has been learned since. Because the truths of ancient times need to be translated into the terms by which we live our own lives—as Paul translated the life of rural, Galilean, Aramaic-speaking Jesus into the terms of the urban, Greek-speaking congregations of Rome and Corinth—theology moves with great discipline, abstraction, and interpretive sensitivity. Because something is always lost in translation and new elements asserted to be true, theology has a grave responsibility to make sure that what is lost is worth losing, for instance an outmoded scientific view, and that what is new is really true, for instance a human place in a universe far vaster than was imagined in biblical times. The unfortunate upshot of all this disciplined care is that theologians often talk only to one another, and few others benefit. Theologians who are employed as deans *have* to preach.

I believe there is a calling for preachers who come to the art from theology itself. We lack the strengths that come to preaching from the other places, but bring the ones that come from theology. These strengths do not include didactic lecturing from the pulpit; that's not a strength. But they do include a large repertoire of images from the long history and diverse cultures of Christianity; an awareness that most claims about the gospel have alternative interpretations that have been defended by well-meaning people; a suspicion of ideologies that insist on one narrow perspective to the exclusion of relevant others; a concern to preach with

11

images that might contradict one another on the surface but cohere and reinforce one another in a deep theological structure; and a sense of humor about how even the most basic images, those that transform the heart, can go awry: The second most frequent response to sermons is misunderstanding (the most frequent response, of course, is sleep).

For too many years I preached lectures, and those sermons were well-received only by those who thought they were getting a break in tuition. About the time I had published enough books to cool the compulsion to lecture, I realized that preaching is an art form, a poetics aimed to transform the hearts of people so as to lead them to be conformed a bit more to the mind of Christ. The transformations are of many kinds, from initial evangelism to meditative deepening of the inner life, just as the mind of Christ is complex. Accordingly there are many kinds of sermons. Sermons are microcosms of the creative Word of God, each intending to make something new, at least a little bit.

By reason of this poetic need, sermons employ both images and arguments, or plot. Arguments need not be logical deductions but consist in the giving of reasons, of showing connections, of presenting juxtapositions, of criticizing mistakes. Human brains are hardwired for images connected with argument. Images alone can set the soul in motion, but without the arguments they lend themselves to wild misinterpretation. Arguments can give clarity to a sermon's intention, but without gripping images do not connect with people's lives and move nothing. Sermons pick up images from religious traditions or from popular culture and give them precision through the arguments that develop them. Most images have been used in other contexts by other people to mean the opposite of what the preacher intends, and only argument can invest them with this sermon's way to the gospel. Only by development through a plot or argument can images move from immediate recognition and nostalgia to a new depth that presents the gospel as new news, evoking greater depth in Christian life. Theologians as preachers can be especially daring with symbols and images because they are self-reflective about the underlying systematic unity that guides the arguments in their sermons. But like any preachers, their images and arguments can carry them far beyond where they initially had intended to go.

The sermons in this book, preached over a three-year period, are grouped according to rough theological topics. Indeed, it is my hope that they offer a way into serious contemporary Christian theology. There are five sections of sermons: *The Evangel* focuses on the call to Christian life, *The Divine Mystery* on the encounter with God, *Jesus Christ* on Christology,

The Church and the World on discipleship, and *Christian Intelligence* on education for discipleship, especially ordained leadership. The distinctions among the topics are only approximate however, matters of emphasis. Nearly every sermon issues an invitation; every one is about God, interpreted Christologically and in terms of some situation in the world; and many are preached in the context of theological education.

Some readers might be more comfortable with other groupings. Footnotes at the end of each provide the information necessary to read them in other orders. In any case I recommend reading the notes before the sermon in order to appreciate the inevitable particular contextuality of their language. Any reader can identify with any of the contexts. The sermons can be read chronologically, although I learn too slowly for three years to make much difference. They can be grouped by preaching context, for instance the matriculation and commencement sermons; the series preached on Sunday mornings in October in the Boston University church, Marsh Chapel, when the Dean of the Chapel, Robert Watts Thornburg, is away celebrating his birthday with his twin brother; the series of Easter Vigil homilies; the series preached in the Chapel of Trinity College, Cambridge; the series preached for the Hebrew Bible class in the School of Theology. These involve different audiences and hence are shaped differently. Or the sermons could be grouped according to the liturgical calendar if one is willing to be broadminded about the Feast of the Matriculation, and so forth.

I am a lectionary preacher, and even the occasional sermons such as for commencement are based on the texts assigned by the Revised Common Lectionary for the day or by the Anglican lectionary in the case of the Trinity College sermons. The only exceptions are the sermons for the Hebrew Bible class whose texts were assigned in the course schedule, and "Thanksgiving," which was designed for the Korean Thanksgiving festival. The lectionary imposes a striking discipline on a preacher, discouraging the indulgence of favorite topics and making for a complex approach to the gospel, which is itself very complex.

My own use of the lectionary is complicated by the frequent appeals to Paul's third letter to Timothy. Those appeals are limited exclusively to sermons for the School of Theology, as that letter is very difficult to find in most Bibles.

The drawings here are by Beth Neville whose art has graced several others of my books. The subjects of the drawings are plants in the Biblical Garden at the Claremont School of Theology where she has twice been artist in residence. The plants are mentioned in the Bible.

Though unrestrained by the faculty, staff, and students of the Boston University School of Theology, I am deeply indebted to them for teaching me most of what I know about preaching. They are biblically centered, theologically wise, committed to the life of the church, forbearing, prudent, and able to fake alertness while sleeping (I noticed!). In gratitude I dedicate this volume to them.

PART ONE
THE EVANGEL

Fig

1. SERPENT POWER

Read and reflect on Numbers 21:4-9, Ephesians 2:1-10, John 3:14-21.

Until today I had thought that the most difficult sermon topic to make attractive is sheep. Little lambs are cute, particularly in cartoons; old sheep are not. I once served a parish in rural Missouri where the highlight of the summer was a mutton barbecue. Every year the church would buy its sheep from one of the two sheep farmers in the congregation; the other farmer would be so angry he would leave the church in a huff until the next year, when he got to sell his sheep to the church and the first farmer would leave angry. Sheep do not always symbolize peace. When Jesus is likened to our shepherd, do you know what that makes us? In ancient art Christians were depicted as a line of sheep following Jesus and the saints in a procession. Do you know what kind of sheep most often comes up for biblical discussion? Lost sheep. The famous prayer begins, "Almighty and most merciful Father, we have erred and strayed from thy ways like lost sheep." Do you know what that means? It means sinning through stupidity, inattentiveness, mindlessness, like sheep cropping along with their heads down not minding the way. The deliberate, conscious, fun sins come up later in the prayer. To think of oneself as a stupid sheep is not uplifting.

But as a sermon topic, sheep beat snakes. As a positive symbol of sacrifice, Jesus can be called the Lamb of God who takes away the sins of the world. Can you imagine Jesus as the Serpent of God who takes away the sins of the world? Actually, I hope you can because that is exactly what our lectionary texts have Jesus say: "And just as Moses lifted up the serpent in the wilderness, so must the Son of Man be lifted up, that whoever believes in him may have eternal life." The very next line from John is the famous statement of salvation: "For God so loved the world that he gave his only Son, so that everyone who believes in him may not perish but may have eternal life." Taken out of context, that line is often interpreted as the sacrifice of Jesus, a sacrifice where Jesus is the sacrificial lamb, an atonement sacrifice. But we see in context that it is not Jesus the sacrificial lamb, it is Jesus the medicinal serpent, the sight of whom prevents death from the snakebite of sin. The lectionary directs us to reflect today on the symbol of serpent power and to see how it contains the gospel.

We should begin, of course, with the Bible's most famous snake, the one in the Garden of Eden (Genesis 3). That snake was beautiful, intelligent, and talkative. It beguiled the human beings to forget their covenant with God. The serpent's speech was not false. If you remember, it said the fruit of the tree was good looking, tasty, and would give you the divine wisdom to distinguish good from evil. All that was true, and having eaten, Adam and Eve knew the difference between good and evil. The problem was not that the serpent lied but that it knew only natural things, the things of nature, and it knew nothing of the special arrangement, the covenant, between God and the people. God's part of the covenant was to provide for the people; and Adam and Eve's part was to care for one another, to cultivate the garden, and to not eat the apple. The snake, with its merely natural truth, beguiled Adam and Eve into forgetting their special covenant with God.

Because this is Lent we have been thinking about how sin is forgetting God at the inopportune times. In the Genesis story God's punishment for sin is to make people mortal, to make cultivation of the earth backbreaking toil, to make childbirth painful, and to make snakes crawl on the ground where they frighten women who always try to kill them. The relations between people and snakes are so problematic that when Isaiah wants to symbolize the miracle of true peace he says not only that the lion shall lie down with the lamb but that human children will play over adders' holes without harm (Isaiah 11:8), an unbelievable miracle.

The snake seems to symbolize something different in the story from Numbers. Remember the context. The Israelites were marching through the wilderness away from Egypt and toward the promised land. The way is desert and hard; there is little water although this incident took place right after Moses got water from the rock and God sent manna from heaven (Numbers 20:2-13; Exodus 16–17). In fact, if the Israelites had remembered, God had liberated them from Egypt, had defeated a large Egyptian army come to take them back into slavery, had led them dry-shod through the Red Sea, and had succored them in every way. But the Israelites did not remember. Like Adam and Eve, they forgot God's covenant. They were beguiled, not by a talking serpent but by the rocky road of life's travels. They blamed God and Moses for taking them from the comforts of Egypt where slavery was still a soft life. And they complained about the dreary dry wilderness and bad food.

How like we are to the Israelites! Our life has good roads and bad roads, good food and bad food. There are times of health and times of sickness, times of prosperity and times of poverty, times when we understand and times when we are confused, times when we accomplish something and times when nothing goes right. In good times it is easy for a grateful people to remember God and give thanks. But in bad times it is tempting to ask God, Why did you do this to us? Why did you bring us here? Where is your protective wing? When we are sick, when it costs more to harvest the crops than to let them rot, or when our children turn out to be trouble, we blame God. Although some pain and tragedy is our own fault, most of it is impersonal misfortune: even worse than blaming God is blaming ourselves as if we were God. That is idolatry. The truth is that life is more often like wilderness than like a promised land. We live on a planet with a molten core whose turbulence quakes the ground, whose climate is uncertain, whose environment is filled with beasts that eat us from without and germs that eat us from within. Nations push one another from one place to another, the Egyptians enslaving Israelites, Israelites driving out Canaanites, Europeans "discovering America" and pushing the Indians onto reservations, Croats, Serbians, and Muslims fighting over Bosnia; Arabs and Israelis fighting over Palestine; Catholics and Protestants fighting over Northern Ireland; Hutus and Tutsis fighting over Rwanda and Burundi. Peoples migrate the way locusts swarm, like a natural force, and no culture stays long in a place it can call its own. Life is more wilderness than promised land, and the world would have more peace if that were recognized.

But just as the Israelites should have remembered that God had brought them out of Egypt to a life of their own, so we should remember that this wilderness is our life. God has given us these years, this place, in which to make our journey. There are better places and times, and there are worse places and times. This is our place and time, and a crucial meaning of faith is the courage to embrace this road. Though it might be better, it might also be worse; and we need to remember God's gift of life with gratitude. To see this life as God's gift brings a deeper joy, a deeper connection with the cosmos and its wilderness, than any easy road, good food, or promised land. But like the Israelites, too often we grouse about the rocks in the path and the bad food.

To complain about life is to ruin the deep joy that surmounts its pain and suffering. You've known people who are chronic complainers. They are so unhappy that life for them is like walking through a yard of snakes. Every pain, every snub, every setback, every loss is like a snakebite. Pretty soon those people who lack the joy of gratitude for life live like those who are dying or are already dead. Maybe life is not a field of real snakes like the Israelites found, but the metaphor is good for some people I know.

Now we come to God's remedy. Moses is told to make a bronze serpent and lift it up on a pole so that all those suffering from snakebite can look at it and live. This symbol has an interesting background. The bronze serpent symbolized an Egyptian minor deity of healing, related to the Greek god of healing, Asclepius. It is from Asclepius that we get our medical symbol of the snake on the pole. Part of what is going on in the story of the Israelites is that God was taking over the Egyptian deity, about whom the Israelites knew and probably worshiped during their long stay in Egypt, and showing that even the false gods could be co-opted for God's purpose.

What is God's purpose? It is to provide a means for life when people in pain remember and look to God. When we are dead in our complaints and life is nothing but snakebites, through the snake comes healing when we look to God and remember with gratitude.

Now we see why Jesus recalled this story. As Paul put it, the entire human race was "dead in its sins," we were "children of wrath." Like the Israelites in the wilderness we could not see the road home because of the dust and rocks and bad food. We try to flee from our lives and their commitments to the escapes of the senses and flesh. Instead of taking our bodies and friends and towns and tasks as gifts for living from God, said Paul, we take them as escapes from God and life. We debase creation because we lack the courage, the faith, to take the road to freedom, and so we die in spirit. For Paul, the image of spiritual death here and elsewhere is a joyless and mechanical devotion to the flesh. We need help, or we shall all die of the snakebite of sin, the sin of forgetting that this path is God's gift.

The help for Christians comes from God in the form of Jesus. Jesus saw himself as a healer, curing many kinds of physical and mental ailments. But even more, he was the physician of the soul. As God turned away the fatal consequences of sin in the wilderness by telling Moses to lift up the serpent, so Jesus saw himself as God's salvation to be lifted up. The early Christians, of course, related this *lifting up* to the cross. The cross means many things besides an instrument of execution, and among them is a simile with Moses' pole for lifting up the saving power of the bronze serpent.

How is it that Jesus heals? The story from Numbers is ancient magic: look at the image of the God and you are healed; in the Greek version of this, to be healed you had to sleep overnight in the temple of Asclepius, hoping that the diseases of the other people who also were sleeping overnight were not contagious. Jesus is more direct. He invites us from the snake pit of sin and spiritual death to join his movement and take part in his ministry. As the Gospel of John says elsewhere (15:1-11), we can join into Jesus' way of life as a cutting can be grafted onto a true vine. Jesus' way of life leads our lives down the path to the promised land, not to a land of milk and honey nor to some tax-free farm with self-harvesting crops, but to God the Father. The Father and I are one, said Jesus (John 10:30). We need to be so close to God that we can love God's gifts of the wilderness life and God's giving of the means to endure without forgetting. Jesus used another image, according to John. I have the water of life, he said; drink of this life and never be thirsty again, no matter how dry and dusty the wilderness road (John 4:13-14).

What is this life of Jesus? All of us here know, but I'll say it again for the sake of good form. It is to love God with an absolute love, more than anything else, more than can be shaken by bad roads, bad food, bad health, bad suffering, bad losses, bad fortune, bad friends. It is to love God with such devotion that as a by-product we love each of God's creatures and see in them the loveliness God put there. We are called to love enemies, because God made them; and we are called to love nature's forces, those things that pain and dislocate and eventually inevitably will kill us, because God made them. Jesus' way is an absolute call to love in a life where everything else is relative and measured. You never can love God enough; it is enough not to fail to love God when called on, when life's demands send us into the wilderness, or to the cross.

You ask how we are to do this. How do we come to Jesus? It's easy enough to look at a bronze serpent on a pole. But how do we come to what Jesus calls "belief in him," which really is this absolute love? Paul says that God's love for us is so persuasive that when we receive it in faith, we can love God back. But this is hard to swallow unless "receiving it in faith" is more than meets the eye. It is. "Receiving Christ in faith" is actually joining up with his movement and devoting oneself to a spiritual life of imitating Jesus' spiritual life, his ministry, his prayers, his honesty, his love.

Therefore, as your preacher, I invite you to come with me to look upon the healing power of the serpent, God's way out of the mortal toxins of forgetfulness, complaining, and escapism. To see Jesus, God's serpent power lifted up, you have to enter into his way of life, join with him and his followers in ministry and a spiritual journey. That way is a wilderness in a creation vaster than we can imagine, deeper than we can feel, more important than we can understand. It requires a lifetime of lessons in loving, of dark nights searching out God's principle, of tiny discernments of God's readiness to bring life forth, of its growth and flourishing and lasting consequences. Jesus' way is subtle, soft, invisible to those who love bright sights, blinding in its illumination, tolerant of failure, reparative of backsliding, transfiguring of ordinary people, transformative of our worst parts, patient over rocky ground, bearing any pressure, enduring any death, bowing to glory, and coming at last to love God with the freedom and joy that are God's own glory and through which we are one body with the world. In this Lenten time I invite you to enter onto this path of healing and wisdom, learning to look at Jesus and see God in whom is your salvation. Amen.

This Lenten sermon was preached in the Claverack Reformed Church in Claverack, New York, on March 13, 1994. My wife and I were married in this church, and our daughter, Gwendolyn Elizabeth, is buried here. On this occasion my mother-in-law, Harriet R. Egan, celebrated her thirty-ninth birthday, again. Like the gospel, it is lighthearted. Also like the gospel, the themes of the stony road and eternal life run deeper than most of the congregation knew.

2. Awake, Thou That Sleepest

Read and reflect on Psalm 17, Ephesians 5:14-17, Matthew 24:36-44.
Hymn: "It Is Well with My Soul," 377; "Stand by Me," 512

Reverend Ellis, members and friends at Columbus Avenue, graduates of Boston University, and members of our community, I greet you in the name of Jesus whose disciples we aim to be, and thank you for the honor and privilege of preaching this morning. You are part of the School of Theology at Boston University in many ways. Now I feel honor bound to confess to you that the first time I preached in an AME Zion church, it closed the next week. But by the grace of God, that church soon reopened under the leadership of one of our graduates, the Reverend Roxie Coicu, and I was able to preach there again at her installation.

The difficulty and importance of bringing the Word of God in a time such as ours are enough to humble any preacher. The November elections demonstrated a mood in this country that is hostile to higher education, hostile to religion except when it is disguised as cheap patriotism, and hostile to minorities such as the African American community with which Boston University long has been closely affiliated. I am here to tell you that Boston University has not fallen prey to the country's mood, that we are more committed than ever to the promotion of the life-changing gospel and to the liberation and flourishing of the African American community, particularly its churches.

This gathering is a testimony not only to the past but, God willing, to the future. Two Great Awakenings to the religion of Jesus that changes the heart have happened in New England, the first in the eighteenth century, the second in the nineteenth. Let the third begin now at Columbus Avenue in Boston.

The November election was not necessary to tell us we live in sorry times. Our people are selfish. Our values are materialistic. And our culture is superficial.

That people are selfish is nothing new. A child's world is very small, almost never expanding beyond what the child does and endures directly. For children, it is hard to see the world from the perspective of anyone else, surely not from the perspective of people much different from them in culture and social class. Many adults never get beyond the stage of children with regard to their selfish perspective on life. Some people, however, become rich, or at least a lot richer than they started, and their selfishness consists in wanting to keep what they have. Not all the rich are selfish, of course. Some are generous and charitable. But the rich have far more reason to protect what they have than the poor who have nothing at all. The most selfish people often are the ones between the rich and poor, those who have a little, often gained at the cost of sacrifice and struggle. They are glad to be no longer poor, but their small gains are easily threatened in tough times; they are the first to slide back to the poverty from which hard work and good luck momentarily have freed them. Those in-between people are the ones who resent the taxes to support welfare for children born out of wedlock to mothers who don't work. They resent the welfare programs that make other people seem more important and deserving than themselves. Blinding themselves to good people sustained by welfare, these in-between people pour their resentment onto scapegoats because they stand so close to that poverty themselves. Of course, not all people who struggle to modest success are selfish, but you can see why the special selfishness of resentment is tempting. It's so close to self-righteousness. In fact, most of us are in between very rich and very poor, and are tempted to this selfishness of upward mobility and terror of the tumble.

I have spoken of selfishness in terms of money, and you know it is far broader. People are selfish for power, and prestige, and love, and for the advancement of their people at the expense of other people. But money is the primary example of the object of selfishness because we are such a materialistic society. People want money so they can buy things and own them. Our values are shaped by television, and television presents the consumer values of corporate sponsors. People value themselves in terms of what they own, what they wear, and what they drive around in. Partly this is because America is a society of people who want to rise in social class, and material goods are the obvious measure of this. Partly it is because the technological innovations of modern life are so wonderful. Partly it is because the highest values, represented usually by religion, seem to be discredited in this century when Christian nations have warred on one another twice and when millions have been gased, atom bombed, and subjected to ethnic cleansing: cynicism about religious hypocrisy often seems to justify materialism.

Selfishness and materialism are ancient faults. The Bible addressed them both. But the ancient world did not know of superficiality as bad as ours. When Jesus attacked materialism by saying, "Lay up for yourselves treasures in heaven" (Matthew 6:19-20), his audience knew what those heavenly treasures were. But we have forgotten. We have forgotten that politics is about justice and think it is only about power. Superficial. We have forgotten that education forms the soul and think it only teaches skills. Superficial. We have forgotten that work is to make a contribution and think it is only to earn a living. Superficial. We have forgotten that economics is to achieve civilization and think it is only about production. Superficial. We have forgotten that art is for enlightenment and think it only should entertain. Superficial. We have forgotten that religion is to make us be like God and think it only should make us feel good. Superficial. We want our actions to have no consequences beyond what we intend, our curiosity to go no farther than what we need; we want our news to be sound bites, our problems to be fixable, our passions to be blind, our friendships to be profitable, our affections cheap, and life easy to understand. This is all superficial and false, my friends, a deceit for the simple, a snare for the sophisticated, a delusion about life, a corruption of civilization, a vain attempt to have it easy. For though life is no longer a garden, God is at its center. We have become selfish and materialistic and superficial and are asleep to the fact that our lives are in the kingdom of God.

If we were to awake and see where we really are, we would see the depths of our problems and the heights of our glories. We would live not for ourselves but for God and our neighbors. We would prize not what rusts but the treasures of heaven. Awake, we would see through power plays to God's justice, through learned skills to God in the soul, through work to the image of God in our creativity, through social wealth to God's destiny for humankind, through entertainment to divine vision, through the fellowship of worship to God's holiness. Should we wake from this sleep, we would see the far reach of our actions, the wonders to be discovered, the complexity of true knowledge, the depths of our problems, the subtlety of passion, the forbearance of friendship, the richness of affection, and the profound mystery of life it takes a lifetime to understand. Lord, wake us from the sin of selfishness and materialism! Wake us from the sleep of superficiality! Wake us, O Lord, to our true condition, to our life in the world, judged, upheld, and surrounded by you! Wake us, O Lord, to the kingdom of heaven at hand! Bring us to the Great Awakening!

Now, of course I am not talking about you. What foolishness to think that the members of Columbus Avenue Church or the alumnae/i and friends of Boston University might be asleep in their sins. White preachers deliver fire and brimstone only to the choir. It's so much safer that way. No, I'm talking only about your neighbors and about the larger society in which we live. And about myself.

Please bear with me for a moment of testimony. I am a professional theologian and think a lot about the things about which I have been talking. As dean of a theological school, I work to define, organize, and inspire the training of potential leaders to carry the wake-up message. I was about fourteen when I gave my life into God's ministry, as I understood it at the time; and I have been ordained for nearly thirty-two years. God has been good to me through all this time. I've been married a week longer than I've been ordained, always to the same woman whose life has flourished, and two of our three children have survived to healthy and well-educated young adulthood. Despite my frequent lapses, God has nourished my soul faithfully with an effective measure of trials and vision, so that for the last year and a half or so, I have been permitted both to glimpse the Glory and to love God as my Beloved, more than I care about God loving me. I don't know anyone else who has received more richly from God, and if I sometimes sound smug and insensitive to the suffering of others, it's because I'm lost in wonder at my own undeserved good fortune.

Yet for all this, to my great shame I go to sleep so easily. I'm selfish and don't realize it until the damage is done. My values are as materialistic as the worst of my neighbors. And I flourish in a culture of superficiality where glibness is more helpful to a dean than the thoughtful expression and exercise of the truth. Though God has waked me time and again, time and again I go to sleep. If I had been at Gethsemane, I would have slept with the others. (Actually, my wife says my snoring might have kept the others awake, so my secret hope is that God can use me even sleeping.)

You see, there is a big difference between salvation on the one hand—which God brings to us with grace abundant and to me in the firm confidence of my heart—and holiness on the other hand, which is our task to work out with God's grace. I am saved in the glory of God, but very much in need of holiness. I praise God, but cry to Jesus to be waked up more often, for longer periods of time. Jesus hears my selfish cries, Jesus listens to my materialist ambitions, Jesus yawns through my superficial blather, and says Wake up! I need to change my ways to keep awake. I need to be less selfish every day, one day at a time. I need to put material things in their proper places, not right in front of me where I like to keep them; and this is a daily struggle. I need to choose the harder path, not the easier, to accept the things I cannot fix or understand, and to engage those things with faith. I am very bad at these steps in holiness and doze off all the time. I need help and encouragement, and mostly perseverance. I ought not sleep while the Lord prays in agony.

So when I call for a Third Great Awakening, its first object is myself. I am the sleeper. What about you? Can you stay awake? Or will you join me in the cry to Jesus for the grace to be awake when he arrives? Will you pray with me for the grace to know when we are being selfish and to stop it? Will you pray with me for the vision to reach for the heavenly treasures and to put material things in their place? Will you pray with me for the hard road, the steep path, for the tasks that reach all the way to God, for the work whose satisfaction we shall not see in this life, for the trials that push our humanity beyond easy achievement, for the call from God that looks at once like light and darkness, height and depth, fullness and abyss, joy and suffering? Will you set yourself now to take the next step in holiness, whatever that means for you? Will you pray with me to wake up more, and stay awake longer?

Then we can awaken our neighborhoods, Boston, New England, the world. We can call out God's waking message, for we have been awakened. We can shine the light on sin and illuminate its selfishness, its materialism, and its superficiality. We can waken our family and friends to our true condition, to its complexity and hardship but also to God's grace abounding.

The line, "Awake, Thou That Sleepest," was used by Charles Wesley as the title of a sermon he preached on April 4, 1742, at the beginning of the First Great Awakening. He and his brother John woke people all over England for fifty years and sent their renewing spirit to America. The Second Great Awakening took place in America in the early nineteenth century, fueling the fires of abolitionism that ended slavery and establishing the Methodist precedent of reaching out to the poor and dispossessed who long for a good word, and engaging them in society, particularly in education. What shall our Third Great Awakening do?

It must engage the poor and dispossessed, to be sure, those hopeless people adrift on city streets and in backwoods hovels, the hopeless people in bondage to drugs, becoming mean in jail, or set on a course of blind violence. But these people, like most of us sometimes, are so needy and desperate they will be turned on by anything yet changed by nothing that lacks the full gospel. A gospel for the poor alone will put them back to sleep and continue the rest of us in the sleep of self-righteousness. The full gospel calls us all to responsibility and holiness. We must address those who are already engaged in society—those who are educated and sophisticated, even those who are rich—regarding their responsibilities. Our whole society is in need of awakening and spiritual renewal, not just the poor and dispossessed. Welfare for the poor does not excuse the rest of us from our responsibilities to neighbors. Like the Good Samaritan (Luke 10:30-37), our responsibility to neighbors is to get them on their feet so that they can be responsible for themselves. And when the poor become responsible, they too care for others less fortunate than themselves.

We live in a culture of victims and payoffs. When we feel sorry for ourselves, we think like victims; and when we feel sorry for others, we like to pay off somebody else to take care of them, preferably a bureaucracy. But the gospel says that we are all sisters and brothers, and that we are to be good loving neighbors to all. We cannot act like victims, and we cannot pay someone else to love for us.

So we must awaken our society, beginning with ourselves and our homes. Holiness does not come easily. But we can break bad habits step by step, we can work together to improve our schools, create good jobs, improve people's health, clean our streets, sanctify our homes, give our children a chance to grow up. God knows, none of these is easy, and it seems sometimes that every step forward leads to two steps back. Every day we must begin again, and the renewal of our society will not be finished until the end of time. If our souls stay awake and struggle for holiness, we shall persevere and overcome. Awake, God is always with us because we live in the kingdom of heaven. Awake, there is no other place than heaven, and there is always grace enough. Awake, we know that in the darkest hour there is still light in the world and the darkness has not overcome it.

Jesus had good words for waking up; listen to their urgency.

The kingdom of heaven is like a thief in the night: stay awake, you householders (Matthew 24:43). The kingdom of heaven is like a king who returns suddenly to demand an accounting from his servants, rewarding those who risked the most and casting out the ones who bury their talents (Matthew 25:14-30). The kingdom of heaven is like a widow who has almost nothing but gives that little to the poor (Luke 21:2-3). The kingdom of heaven is like a mustard seed that looks like nothing but when planted grows into a tree in which birds can take their rest (Mark 4:30-32). The kingdom of heaven is like a sower who scatters seed, some to grow and others to die or be trampled (Mark 4:1-20). The kingdom of heaven is like a rich parent who welcomes home the worst of children and helps the best of children receive grace humbly (Luke 15:11-32). The kingdom of heaven is like a ruler who gives a wedding banquet for the prince and invites all who can to come to the feast but throws into the outer darkness the person whose clothing shows he did not know where he was (Matthew 22:1-14). The kingdom of heaven is like a wedding party waiting for the bridegroom, some of whom are ready and others of whom are not (Matthew 25:1-13). The kingdom of heaven is like the people before the Flood, when only Noah was ready. "Two will be in the field; one will be taken and one will be left. Two women will be grinding meal together; one will be taken and one will be left. Keep awake therefore, for you do not know on what day your Lord is coming" (Matthew 24:36-42).

If you would be holy and bring justice to our land, then wake up now and carry the word, for there is not a moment to lose. My friend, the fields are ripe for the harvest and the laborers are few. Let us put down our dreams of contentment, our selfish preoccupations, resentments, defensiveness, and greed; our materialistic concerns for show, possessions, and status; our superficial pleasures and accomplishments; and enter onto the path of holiness. Let us take up God's work to awaken our neighbors, to bring justice rolling down like waters, to fix what we can and struggle to make manifest God's kingdom. Though we cannot become holy overnight, we can become holier tomorrow than we are today. Though we have no guarantee of success in this life, we have the guarantee of grace equal to every need. Though we cannot awaken everyone with strong words, we can awaken those next to us who listen. When the Great Awakening begins here and goes out into the world, it shall be stormy and filled with tribulations. We will have faults and failures, and the stronger we are the more we shall be persecuted. But when we come to the end of our strength and the work is still not done, we will find our Lily of the Valley, our Beloved, our God (Song of Solomon 2: 1-2). I invite you to pray for me and one another to stay awake and receive the Great Commission to awaken the world. For we have Jesus with us. Stand with me to call to him,

"When the storms of life are raging, stand by me." Amen.

The Boston University School of Theology has a long tradition of educating African American church leaders. The occasion for this sermon, at the Columbus Avenue AME Zion Church in Boston, on February 19, 1995, was to honor our African American graduates. The Reverend Michael Ellis was pastor. To preach a new Great Awakening there was presumptuous of me. But one has to start somewhere. I concluded by singing Tindley's great hymn, "When the Storms of Life Are Raging, Stand by Me," p. 512 in The United Methodist Hymnal.

3. WATCH FOR THE LIGHT

Read and reflect on Isaiah 2:1-5, Romans 13:11-14, Matthew 24:36-44.

Divine light is dangerous, but demanding—and the ultimate reward. Like the creation, it has but one source. When it catches us, the question is whether it shines through, setting us aglow, or reflects itself back casting our shape as a shadow. That question sets the problem of judgment, incarnation, and holiness: the topics of Advent.

The passage from Isaiah gives little hint of the complexity and ambiguity of the divine light. The house of God on Zion shall be lifted up "in days to come," said Isaiah, and "all the nations shall stream to it." From that place (that is no place) in that time (that does not come), God shall be our teacher of righteousness, the judge and arbiter among peoples, and the peacemaker whose instruction does not include the arts of war. The passage concludes, "O house of Jacob, come, let us walk in the light of the LORD!"

As if walking in the light of the Lord were easy! Isaiah placed it in a kind of dream time and space. In his narrative the promise of peace is sandwiched between a condemnation of Jerusalem as a whore and an accusation of the house of Jacob as having given itself over to idols. Six verses after the end of our Advent passage Isaiah wrote, "the LORD alone will be exalted on that day."

The condition for "walking in the light of the Lord" is a general acknowledgement of God as the righteous king, who is also peacemaker, judge, and teacher, an acknowledgment that must have seemed as distant in Isaiah's day as in ours. But you can understand how the Christian designers of the lectionary could take this passage to prefigure the messiah. Up until the days of Samuel the judge, Yahweh had considered himself King of Israel, ruling through the judges who led the people in battle. In Samuel's last great battle against the Philistines, the Lord stepped in to thunder "with a mighty voice" that threw the enemy into confusion (1 Samuel 7:10). But when Samuel got old and his sons did not look promising, the people demanded a flesh and blood king to rule properly for Yahweh on earth (1 Samuel 8). Reluctantly, Samuel anointed Saul, who did not work out, and then David, who did. The anointed kings, or messiahs, were human surrogates for Yahweh, the heavenly king, and were pledged to bring peace and uphold justice, caring particularly for the poor and weak. The model of Messiah as righteous king was one of the central images by which Jesus was understood in his generation, however much he modified the model.

In expectation, then, of the advent of Jesus Christ—the divine light who came into the world, the light that is the life of all people, the light that shines in the darkness and the darkness does not overcome it, the true light, the light that enlightens everyone—let us hope for the man who is the divine king. Let us hope for the reign of righteousness in which the poor shall be lifted up, the weak given strength, the sick healed, the lame made to walk, the deaf made to hear, and the blind made to see. Let us hope for the kingdom of God ruled by a Messiah of justice who decides between claims with wisdom, who restores the earth to be a garden for all, who instructs us in the arts of life and not death. Let us hope for a ruler of our hearts who will bring truth, not self-deception; who will let us see others as they are, not as we have need to classify them; who will forgive us and teach us to forgive others. Let us long for a peacemaker whose people can "beat their swords into plowshares, and their spears into pruning hooks" so that "nation shall not lift up sword against nation, neither shall they learn war any more" (Micah 4:3). Let us hunger and thirst for the day when we can say to one another, "Come, let us walk in the light of the Lord." For the Advent of the Messiah, the Light of the World, is upon us.

Now Advent comes every year, and we do not live in the dream time of the once and future king. Let us demythologize the Romance-of-King-Arthur version of the Messiah at once. Whereas most of the Jews of Jesus' generation expected a Messiah to be a real king and bring about the reign of righteousness, Jesus obviously did not do that. Things were as bad as before; they got worse by 70 C.E. when the temple was destroyed, and utterly disastrous by 134 when Jewish national identity was destroyed. When we look around, we see progress in education and medicine, but not religion;

progress in technology and human rights, but not religion; progress in institutions of social responsibility, but not the religion of the human heart. More people in our time than ever before are rich in the sense of having access to education, medicine, media communication, and means of livelihood; but also more people in our time than ever before are denied those things. We suffer more poverty, violence, abuse, hunger, homelessness, and human callousness than ever before. No righteous king has amended our world, and we are reminded of that each Advent. A dispassionate observer might suggest abandoning the whole Messiah movement and returning to the twice-removed rule of the old judge walking from high place to high place with the ark of the covenant.

Jesus himself demythologized the Arthurian view of the Messiah with devastating words:

> But about that day and hour no one knows, neither the angels of heaven, nor the Son, but only the Father. For as the days of Noah were, so will be the coming of the Son of Man. For as in those days before the flood they were eating and drinking, marrying and giving in marriage, until the day Noah entered the ark, and they knew nothing until the flood came and swept them away, so too will be the coming of the Son of Man. Then two will be in the field; one will be taken and one will be left. Two women will be grinding meal together; one will be taken and one will be left. Keep awake therefore, for you do not know on what day your Lord is coming. But understand this: if the owner of the house had known in what part of the night the thief was coming, he would have stayed awake and would not have let his house be broken into. Therefore you also must be ready, for the Son of Man is coming at an unexpected hour. (Matthew 24:36-44)

Note that the advent will not be historical in the sense of coming at the right time, at the kairos. It will be at the wrong time, wholly unexpected, and like the people in the days of Noah, we shall know nothing until the flood comes and sweeps us away. The advent will not be the end of time, because two will be working and one will be taken while the other works on, hoping for next year's advent. Nor will the advent bring a reign of prosperity and plenty; rather, it will be like a thief in the night who steals your household goods. Jesus' metaphors for himself are hardly those easily attached to the righteous king. Jesus is like a devastating flood, an arbitrary kidnapper, and a sneak-thief. Mark's version of this parable (13:24-37) is slightly more benign: a householder returns suddenly at

33

night to see whether the slaves are napping; Luke's version is worse than Matthew's, adding Lot's experience in Sodom and Gomorrah as a parallel to Noah, with the Son of Man coming like brimstone (Luke 12).

Some people read Jesus' sayings like these as apocalyptic warnings of the end of the world. But that seems to me to inflate hyperbole with more hyperbole. Jesus was rather talking dramatically about divine judgment on persons and peoples. It's like saying that you do not know when your life will be required of you, perhaps before morning, perhaps while working; perhaps a flood will remove a people, or fire and brimstone a town. The problem is that we are unready for judgment when business is usual, when we eat and drink, marry and are given in marriage. Suddenly the king comes, stops everything, and asks "Where is your righteousness? Why are there homeless people on your steps? Why are you in competition with nations poorer than yourselves? Why are so many tax dollars going to armaments? Why are children hungry, uneducated, unemployed, and reduced to crime? Why do you think your race is better than others? Why do you harbor anger against people because of their gender? Why are your habits petty when your wealth is generous? Why are you selfish when you could reach out? Why do you sell out to your passions when you could focus them on being somebody? Why do you let life wash you along when you live before God? Why are you silent in life's inertia when you could sing God's praise? Why do you let your mind flip from channel to channel when you could be praying? Why do you eat, drink, and be merry," asks the king, "for tomorrow you die." You never know, said Jesus, when you will be called to judgment. Watch out for it.

Death is a graphic incident of judgment. But we are under judgment all the time. For most of us there is tomorrow, and we can make amends and be able to give a good account to the king's questions. But that is really beside the point. Tomorrow has its own agenda, sufficient for that day. Each time is a new creation, and we must start from where we begin in that time and live before God as beloved creatures, respecting one another, honoring our natural home, and amending our institutions so as to fit the righteous kingdom. As for the past, it is fixed and gone and the only thing to be done for its failures is to seek forgiveness: first admit the truth about ourselves in judgment, then throw ourselves on God's mercy, and give it up.

Here is the Christian innovation for the Messiah. God comes not with strength of arms to enforce righteousness but with forgiveness and love. With divine love, as Bonaventure saw, we can open our eyes in the blinding light of judgment and see who we are without denial. With divine love, as Calvin saw, we can accept the condemnation of our sins and the justice of God or life in meting out any pain whatsoever. With divine love, as Tillich saw, we can accept ourselves as accepted by God because God has made us lovelier than we can ruin. With divine love we can forgive ourselves and neighbors, forget our sins because they are behind us, and take up life with the new chance this day brings.

Jesus was the new Messiah because he brought God's forgiving love into the world and shared it with Mary and Martha, Peter and John. Philip took it to Africa, Thomas to India, and Paul to Europe. From Stephen the Martyr to Martin Luther King, Jr., saints have witnessed to that love when the old-fashioned rule of sword and spear seemed more attractive. There are not many Christophers, Christ-bearers, in the world today, though many go by that name. But someone, some act, some book, carried Christ's love to you and brought you here to carry it on. Someone, some act, some book, put a spark of divine light into your soul and the darkness has not prevailed against it: fan that flame so that you will come aglow, light the path of those around you, climb Zion's hill so that you will enter a city that lights the world.

Paul said, "You know what time it is, how it is now the moment for you to wake from sleep. For salvation is nearer to us now than when we became believers; the night is far gone, the day is near. Let us then lay aside the works of darkness and put on the armor of light." The dream time and space, said Paul, is not some mythic future place but rather our present life as sleepwalkers. Even we who are believers are dreaming now, said Paul. Wake up to the morning light of true time and space! As dreaming we pursue business as usual; were we awake, we would find ourselves under judgment. As dreaming, we are imprisoned by vague guilts and generalized self-condemnations as in a bad dream; were we awake, we would see with crystalline light our true faults and merits. As dreaming, we are slaves to our sinful habits, those of our society and those of our own making; as in a nightmare running up a slippery hill, even our sinful acts are not wholly our own, and the little good we do is of God's origin; were we awake, we would see the light of God's love within us setting the power of those sins in the past and directing us to the time at hand. As dreaming, we think that the powers of the world must sweep aside our puny efforts and that no effort is worth it; were we awake, we would see that salvation comes from God, not from our efforts, and that the power of our lives is divine light-power.

35

"Stay awake and be ready," said Jesus. "Wake up now," said Paul, "for the night is over and the light of day is dawning." What shall we see when the light dawns? What do we look for every Advent when the light that enlightens every person is expected to return yet again? With fear and trembling we look for judgment, for only in the light with which God sees us can we see God. Judgment is the only door to salvation. With faith and hope we look for forgiveness and love so that we can live thankfully before God. When we awake to the presence of the king of love, we can indeed "walk in the light of the Lord." For when we have passed from sleep to waking, we know that our true time, our numbered set of days, is in the eternity of God and that our true place, our field of battle, of duty and love, is only in God's immensity. We are real only within the power of God's creative act, and the illusion that we can exist apart from God, where God can be kept at a distance or postponed, is only a dream that enslaves. The divine light of salvation shines through us and makes us incandescent. There are not real shadows. Only in dreams do we cast shadows. But the dreams are real enough when we are asleep.

Come, Lord Jesus, and awaken us. Shine your light upon us so that we may work in the day to nurture the kingdom of righteousness. Where we cast shadows, heat us hotter with the glow of your love. Where we cannot see life's meaning, cast your light a little farther. Forgive our drowsy dreaming and open us at last to the pure light of creation in which you glorify our time within eternity and our place within immensity. Glory be to you in whom we live and move and have our being. Immanuel. Amen.

It was my privilege to preach this Advent sermon at the chapel service of the Boston University School of Theology on December 3, 1992, in Marsh Chapel. The theme of apocalyptic time and eternity is introduced here, as well as the divine immensity or unmeasurableness; for a more theoretical approach, see my Eternity and Time's Flow *(Albany: SUNY Press, 1993).*

4. NAILED TO THE CROSS

Read and reflect on Hosea 1:2-10, Colossians 2:6-15, Luke 11:1-13.
Hymns: "Holy, Holy, Holy," 64; "It Is Well with My Soul," 377;
"Come, O Thou Traveler Unknown," 386

Jesus said, "Ask, and it will be given you; search, and you will find; knock, and the door will be opened for you. For everyone who asks receives, and everyone who searches finds, and for everyone who knocks, the door will be opened." These words are not obviously true. Nearly every one of us has prayed for money at some time or other to meet some need that seemed desperate, and rarely have we come into extraordinary windfalls. Everyone has prayed for the ability to do or perform something; I think it was Dick Gregory who said that so long as they teach arithmetic, there will be prayer in schools. Despite asking, searching, and knocking few of us are superstars or geniuses. Some of us, a very great many I suspect, have sought for healing, for relief from pain and suffering, or for the saving of our children, to no avail. So Jesus' words are not about an automatic connection between human petition and divine response. Most prayers are not answered, at least as asked. On the other hand, there is truth in the old saying that you should be careful what you pray for because you might get it.

Jesus' words, of course, are about the search for God, not money, success, or health. But the search for God means different things at different stages in that search, and so both the meaning of searching and the meaning of the God on whose door we knock change with the stages on the journey. The spiritual life of individuals and communities is almost infinitely complicated, but I want to lift up for consideration three stages here.

The beginning stage is when we ask what God can do for us today. This is the beginning because we do not have to know much about God at all.

We just have to hurt, to be needy, to be trapped, to feel powerless and at our wit's end. This stage of spiritual life seems less about God than about ourselves. Most people in our society do not even think of God when they and their lives need fixing, only about themselves. They are hurt, anxious, depressed, or bored. They despair of significant achievement or meaningful life. So they abandon hope, they quit the struggle, they give in to the powers of corruption and inertia, and unconsciously they choose to die. Go to the shopping malls and you will find large crowds who think that buying something will give them life. Go to any large office and you will find people who think they might as well join the prevailing exploitation because resistance would cost them that success which counterfeits for life. Go to the street corners in our city and you will see men and women of all ages who prey upon their neighbors, who waste their own lives, and who make their neighborhoods little hells to hurt the weak and seduce the innocent, all because they have given up hope that real life is something better. Check your sofas, and you might find a couch potato who has died to life in pale hope of entertainment.

We Christians have good news for these people: God can do something for you today! You can have new life. You can hope in God, and that will transform everything. Your life might be dangerous, but you need not be anxious because it is in God's hands. Your circumstances might be painful and getting worse, but you can live through all that, the pain, loss, even death, and come to God in the end. You can embrace the people, the forces, and the diseases that will kill you because your hope is firm that God wins in the end. You can resist the evil that permeates your neighborhood, witnessing to the good, because however many skirmishes we lose, we know that God fights the last battle. We Christians need to tell the world that God is here, that the unwitting choice to die is sin, that sin is losing hope, and that because of Jesus our hopelessness is nailed to the cross. No matter how bad things get, God is with us. And when we understand that fact, we are reborn to new life.

What can God do for you today? God can give you new life and hope to face all that life brings with the vast love and energy of the Creator. And God gives you a community of people struggling with new life like yourself, a community to hold and help you, and to use the help you yourself can give. Then when circumstances defeat our projects, and we get tired, old, and lose our powers, we come to realize that the life and energy we have enjoyed all along is God's anyway, and that it goes on in God's world undiminished.

Now you surely will tell me that this beginning stage of spiritual life is childish and selfish. True enough. It is childish, magical thinking to believe that God will throw money your way instead of you having to work for it, or that God will heal your sickness instead of your going to the doctor, or that God will end the evils that shape our society instead of our struggling through hard and ambiguous changes. What God will do is give you the strength to bear up and the hope to take life as a gift and love it all, the good and bad and ambiguous together.

As to the selfishness of asking what God can do for us today, that's only half the story. The other half is that God loves us when we are selfish; and if we take our hope seriously, we will take everything to God. When we give ourselves over to God, there is nothing we should hold back, no need or desire, no matter how childish or selfish. If you need money, go to work but also ask God, for otherwise you hide your heart. If you are sick, find a doctor but also pray for healing, for otherwise you temper your hope in God. If your life can't get started, is a failure, corrupt, mired in evil, or destructive, work to correct it but pray steadily and with many tears for help, for otherwise you are choosing death if things do not work out your way. God nails our hopelessness to the cross and returns our life to us renewed if only we ask, search, and knock. Sing "Fix me, Jesus," sing it often, and let God worry about the fact we are still selfish sinners.

If we beat on God's door long enough, we will be confronted with the fact that God is more glorious than our needs are hurtful. Most of us who search for God at some time encounter God's holiness. We sang "Holy, Holy, Holy" at the beginning of our service, and most organized religion is organized in response to God's holiness. If the first stage in the spiritual search is to ask what God can do for us, the second stage is to ask what we can do for God today. The shorthand word for this part of spiritual life is *ministry*: We minister in order to do God's work in the world. If you have ever been deeply involved in the life of a Christian congregation, or a Jewish, Muslim, or Buddhist congregation for that matter, you know how many parts that ministry has. There is the ministry of visiting the sick and imprisoned, of comforting people in grief or pain, of establishing a program of activities within the congregation so that people learn more forgiving and uplifting ways of getting along, including ways of searching out God's path. There are also ministries to the hungry, the poor, and the mentally ill in one's neighborhood, and ministries of social justice that seek cooperation with others to effect changes in unjust conditions. There are ministries of support for people who are pushing themselves to accomplish great things, such as artists and athletes, and ministries of support for the little people like most of us who mean no more than to be kind and move through life without interfering too much. All these and other ministries are expressions of the more basic ministry of helping God's life-giving love grow and become more effective. What God can do for us is give us hope in life. What we can do for God is give God's restorative love life in the world, increasing hope. Another word for *ministry* is worship, with both indoor liturgy and outdoor effort.

Why is it so hard to do something for God? You would think that the point of giving ourselves to ministry, in thanksgiving and awe at God's holiness, is so obvious that the kingdom of God would be coming in faster than the Internal Revenue Service can keep track of capital gains. But most churches are struggling to maintain basic ministries. Some churches are bursting with new members but find that the enthusiasms cool quickly. Too many churches are dependent on a few saints who seem to be called on for every ministry. Why does doing something for God need constant cheerleading?

Paul addressed the problem obliquely in the Colossians passage. Speaking of our sinful selves, he said we were "dead in trespasses." That is what I meant before in talking about the hopelessness that chooses death through anxiety, evil, and giving in to disease and pain. On the one hand are the specific evils that we do, and on the other is the great evil, true sin, that consists in hopelessness for authentic life itself. Hopelessness is the denial of God and God's power to give us a life that bears through all things. That sin, that huge sin of hopelessness and denial, is a cause for pervasive and profound guilt. So when, for us as beginners, God gives us new life and hope and starts us out on the spiritual path, we still are weighed down by the guilt of having chosen death before. We now have hope and a new start, but that fragile new life carries such a great weight of guilt.

Then, should we be so fortunate as to encounter the holy God, to be filled with awe at God's majesty and glory, how much heavier does that make the weight of sinful guilt! How could we ever have loved death? How could we have failed in hope? In the face of God's holy mystery, we suddenly realize how bad things were before. Before, we thought we only hurt and were needy. Now we see that we were profoundly blasphemous.

How hard it is to keep on track with this new life and its ministries of God's work when we are weighed down by guilt! Of course we are new people now, filled with hope, full of thanksgiving for what God has done for us and of awe at God's glory. But this is so hard to remember sometimes.

We bend around our guilt to distort God's gifts of new life and visions of holiness into subtle new accusations against us. And so our enthusiasms for ministry peter out, we come to church less often, work less hard, and finally develop Sabbath morning enthusiasms for soccer as a family value.

Wrong, said Paul, "When you were dead in trespasses . . . God made you alive together with him, when he forgave us all our trespasses, erasing the record that stood against us with its legal demands. He set this aside, nailing it to the cross." God has come for you, given you new life, and taken away your sins. You carry them only if you take them back, and that is a stupid, death-loving, thing to do. No matter how bad you are even today, how unreformed and still framed by the habits of death, you are accepted by God who has nailed your sins to the cross. Nothing need hold us back from God's ministry, from doing everything we can for God, unless we hoist our guilt off the cross and neurotically shoulder it again. The more we understand, the clearer it is that our guilt is not just draped on the cross but nailed there. Forget it, and get to work.

There is one more segment of the journey of asking, searching, and knocking for God that I want to mention. But I do it with hesitancy because I fear few people will understand. Please consider this just my personal testimony if it seems strange. Although we never get beyond the need to ask God to fix us, and although we never complete the ministries that we can do for God, I do think that as God moves toward us these things become like bright lights that are made to seem pale by an even brighter light. They are still definitive of who we are but not as important as something else, because who we are is not as important as something else. The brighter light, the something else beyond who we are is our loving God, loving God fully, being filled with the bliss of adoring God, being so filled with adoration that our being done for and our doing for are relatively trivial. Leading our lives is important; yes, but loving God is something else again, and it takes your breath away.

There are many good forms of loving God that I do not mean here. I do not mean loving God for doing something for us. Nor do I mean loving God as the source and object of our own ministries and labors. What I mean is the emotional vision of God as infinite beyond all creatures, of God the abyss of deep formless creativity from which arises all forms, of God the Light that plays on us as delightful creatures, of God whose presence makes our eyes roll up and our lips smile a silly grin, of God the deep, swift river that beckons us across to Glory. That vision is bliss and in it God is our beloved.

How do we move to the stage of this vision and love? I think it is like Horatio Spafford's expansion of Paul's point in his hymn we just sang: "My sin, not in part but the whole, is nailed to the cross, and I bear it no more, praise the Lord, praise the Lord, O my soul!" My sins are all in parts, and I would be pleased to have them one by one nailed to the cross. But the whole of sin is infinitely frightening. It is the infinite Nothingness in me, and in you. And when the whole of our sin is nailed to the cross, we are in God's land, not our own. When the whole of our sin is nailed to the cross, we can't cry for help, we can't work for God, we can only adore. For in the end, as in the beginning, there is only God, in whom we are privileged to delight for the quick flash of our lives.

So I invite you to pray for what God can do for us today and to tell others who hurt that God can do something for them too. I invite you to join me in the Christian movement to do something for God, the Holiest of Holies whom we worship and whose world needs our ministries. And when you come through that, I also invite you to submit to the transformation of soul, the abandonment of self, the release of seriousness into humor, that opens the door to loving God. God is creator, judge, and redeemer, but most of all, the Lily of the Valley, most ready to be our beloved when we are called to the vision.

> And, Lord, haste the day when my faith shall be sight,
> the clouds be rolled back as a scroll;
> the trump shall resound, and the Lord shall descend,
> even so, it is well with my soul.
> (Horatio G. Spafford, *The United Methodist Hymnal,* 377)

During the summer months, the Sunday morning services at Boston University are conducted by the Reverend Anthony Campbell. He was gracious to allow me to preach on July 30, 1995. The hymns are important for the sermon, and in fact I sang the verse at the end.

5. Thanksgiving

Read and reflect on Psalm 103.

Bless the LORD, O my soul, and all that is within me, bless his holy name." I wish with all my heart that my life could be a blessing song to God. If you asked Pastor Lee, I wager he would say that his ministry would be fulfilled if all of you blessed the Lord with all that is in you. Thanksgiving begins when we become aware in gratitude of how God blesses us. But thanksgiving becomes truly real only when we rise up to bless God.

The psalmist reminds us that thanksgiving is not as simple as we might think. The initial impulse to establish Thanksgiving as a holiday comes from gratitude for a good harvest. Most of us city people are not many generations from the farm. As a child I spent summers helping my grandfather milk cows; actually, although he said I helped, I think he really was showing love by tolerating this city boy who knew nothing useful about cows or harvest. But I learned the importance of harvest: this was the source of food and life.

The harvest is itself a metaphor for all the benefits we receive from God. We are thankful for work, for peace, for children, for schools, for increasing productivity, for friends from abroad, for a nation that grows stronger with each crisis, for people who know us and our faults and still love us, for churches that bring us together and teach us the words to sing praises—no one would be here this morning if they did not have some blessing from God that harvests God's love. "Bless the Lord, O my soul."

Yet the psalmist knows as well as we that *these* blessings from God are not the real thing. They come and they go, like the flowers of the field when the wind passes over and they are gone. You and I have been unemployed. We have known war. Only two of my three children are alive today. We remember economic depressions. Foreign friends are not always helpful. Governments sometimes grow more corrupt than strong in virtue. Some folks see our faults and hate us. Our church sometimes stumbles into self-serving and wickedness. Sometimes we sing hypocrisy rather than blessing. The world has not only material benefits but physical and psychological suffering, and the psalmist knew that. The benefits we want for ourselves are the good life; but God offers something different.

Recall again with me the benefits the psalmist listed: forgiveness of our iniquity; healing of diseases; redemption from death and forgetting; love and mercy; renewal of strength when the savor of good things fades to blandness, blindness, and silence; vindication and justice for the oppressed; knowledge of God's deeds; a time limit on divine judgment; divine love that is as great as the heavens are high above the earth; God's knowledge that we are little more than dust and that too much cannot be expected of us.

Whereas we want peace, prosperity, comfort, and happiness for our children, God offers us the satisfaction that he knows that nothing good lasts forever and that we love ourselves more than God, that our hearts can go bad no matter how good they are when they start, and that life can be one grief after another. And knowing this, God still loves us through all the turns of fortune's wheel—good and bad, when we are happy and when we mourn, when we remember to thank God and also when we curse God for our misfortunes and expel him from our memory. Through all this, even through our iniquities, God loves us, sings the psalmist. "The steadfast love of the LORD is from everlasting to everlasting." We and our fortunes change, but God abides forever.

So thanksgiving is for these strange benefits, for God's love that accepts our faults and also tolerates our suffering. We are gone from the Garden, the ground is hard, labor is painful, the world is dangerous, we die too soon, and even the roses in our path trick us with thorns. But God loves us with an everlasting love.

Let me sharpen the tension the psalmist draws. There is a vast distance between God and us. God is the infinite creator who has established his throne in the heavens and whose kingdom rules over all. We are made of dust and are short-lived. Yet God loves us, and we are supposed to bless, that is, to love God. How can love and blessing cross that vast distance? Perhaps it is not a problem for God. God's infinite and everlasting love can cross any distance. Moreover, God's love cannot be turned aside by our own wickedness, faithlessness, and failure to love in return. God's love just brushes that aside and embraces us however and wherever we are. God's love came to us in Jesus and will draw us home.

But how are we to love and bless God? When things are going well, thanksgiving, love, and blessing are easy enough. But God no more makes for us an easy, pleasant world than we always present ourselves spotless before our maker. What comfort is it to know that God will conquer evil and vindicate the oppressed in the long run when we and our loved ones suffer now? I am pleased that God forgives my iniquities, but I would rather that my daughter had the chance to live a full life. Can you bless God with your whole heart when you take into account the ambiguous world we live in?

My friends, the Christian path is to learn how to bless the Lord with all our soul and to find divinity in the evil and suffering of our lives, as well as the fat harvests of material benefits. This is the path of holiness, as Wesley called it, and I invite you onto it if you are not already on the way. We begin as children on the path by concentrating on the good things and ignoring the bad. Then we mature to see through the material benefits and sufferings of life to the important benefits the psalmist mentions: the benefits of God's everlasting love and forgiveness. Then we move on down the path past the point of asking what God can do for us to ask what we can do for God: here our blessing of God is active service and ministry. I presume that the life of blessing in this congregation is mainly at this stage of loving God through service and ministry. As Jesus blessed the Father by giving himself for us, we bless God by continuing Jesus' ministry and service.

But there is more to blessing God than service, even though we should never abandon that. We should love and bless God, not for what he does for us but because of who God is. I pray that we can rise together to a vision of God's holiness, to love God the Creator of the cosmos, the creator of space and time, who holds our future, our past, and our present together in eternity, and whose life pulses with an energy that makes our time-bound lives seem one-dimensional. We have a path, my friends, that leads to the throne. Let us start the path with gratitude, walk its steep steps in service, and then run home to the throne at the end with praise, giving over our hearts to nothing but blessing:

> Bless the Lord, O you his angels, you mighty ones who do his bidding, obedient to his spoken word. Bless the Lord, all his hosts, his

ministers that do his will. Bless the Lord, all his works, in all places of his dominion. Bless the Lord, O my soul, and all that is in me bless his holy name. Amen.

Thanksgiving is, of course, the proper response to the gospel, the evangel. This sermon was preached in the Sang Dong Methodist Church in Seoul, Korea, where the Reverend Dong Hak Lee is pastor, on November 26, 1995. It was translated line by line in the service by Dr. Peter Sun, a Boston University School of Theology alumnus.

PART TWO
THE DIVINE MYSTERY

Lemon

6. LOST SHEEP IN THE DIVINE IMMENSITY

Read and reflect on Romans 6:3-11, Psalm 114, Matthew 28:1-10.

The time of the Easter Vigil is weird, suspended between crucifixion and resurrection. In our deeply human fear that resurrection might not be the outcome of crucifixion in our case, we intensify the symbols of identity in this service. Not content to repeat that Christ is the Light of the World, we bring in lights ourselves just in case. Not content to profess faith that God can save us, we recite story after story from Scripture of God's powers of liberation. Not resting easy that our Christian identity is shaped by the conjunction of crucifixion and resurrection, we celebrate both baptism and Eucharist as if Christian identity needs reinforcement. The lectionary texts for this sermon are framed with accounts of divine immensity, divine unmeasurableness according to normal terms: in Psalm 114 God makes the mountains skip around like sheep, in Matthew God sends an angel who scares the guards half to death and raises Jesus from death itself. Between these frames of divine immensity is Paul's word that we already have died to sin in baptism and already have been raised to new life in God, already have been taken out of human measure into God's immensity, and therefore are not in truth waiting around Saturday night anxious about the reality of Easter. Nothing is normal tonight. The symbols are too intense and too many. The words go on and on as if none ever says a believable finished truth. We're supposed to be waiting, but we cram the time with the activities peculiarly Christian: processing, preaching, reciting, singing, sacraments. As if this hovering between death and life prompts us to clutch at the signs of identity because here there is no comprehensible measure of finite identity. As if here human measures are

49

only shadows and the reality is divine immensity. *Immensity,* you know, is the Latinate word that means unmeasured, that which transcends limits, explodes categories, and consumes signs. Immensity is spooky because we do not know where we are, or even who anymore. Between crucifixion and resurrection, the Easter Vigil is spooky and our frenetic Christian business is whistling hymns in the immense darkness.

I call attention to this background in order to make you feel relieved that I am going to talk about sin. Under ordinary circumstances, a sermon about sin is an embarrassment to liberals, a source of false righteousness to conservatives, and a threat to everyone else. At the Easter Vigil, however, sin is a welcome comic relief.

Let me urge you now to bracket temporarily your meditation on the immense uncertain suspension between crucifixion and resurrection and think instead of the fact that today is the last day of Lent. Lent begins well enough with Mardi Gras and Ash Wednesday, but nearly always fizzles out in its end with the higher drama of the cross and grave. Contrary to popular piety, Good Friday is not the culmination of the season of penance; today is. There is nothing like the remembrance of our own sins to bring back finite measure when faced with the divine immensity.

The prayer of confession from the 1928 *Book of Common Prayer* describes our situation this way: "Almighty and most merciful [God], We have erred and strayed from thy ways like lost sheep. We have followed too much the devices and desires of our own hearts. We have offended against thy holy laws. We have left undone those things which we ought to have done; And we have done those things which we ought not to have done; And there is no health in us."

For most of my Christian life I have resented the analogy with sheep. But now that I have responsibility for learned ministry in this institution, the point of the analogy has become clear. Sheep are stupid. They cannot keep track of anything long range and need a shepherd—that was the offensive part of the analogy. So they wander off the path and out of sight with no motive but proximate smell of tantalizing grass and dew-filled hollows. Sheep do not intend to get lost. They do not intend to annoy their shepherds, nor to lord it over their ninety-nine companions by attracting special attention. They just wander off and thereby ruin their own and everyone else's safe passage to the good pasture or back home.

Ninety percent of our sins, starting with Adam and Eve's, are stupid sheep sins. We have no specially wicked motive. We are not bound down by intractable bad habits. We just do not think. We do not keep our eye on the goal. We do not watch to see how to keep up with and help the rest. We do not pay attention to advice or leadership. We act as if we were asleep or mindlessly munching. From mindless straying comes catastrophe. We blunder into the den of wolves or over the precipice or into someone else's fight, and wake up to see that we are lost and in trouble. Half our companions have followed us into this danger. And the lifelines back to home are out of sight. Thus we are committed to living the life of sin, trying to win or beat it, sleepily aware that what we see is what we have, awaking to the need to get along on our own.

So we come to the devices and desires of our own hearts, all we have left after our stupid sheeplike straying. Following the devices and desires of our hearts is perilously close to freedom. Spinoza defined it exactly as freedom, with bondage being a coercion to do something contrary to one's will. Every critic has noted that Milton's Satan in *Paradise Lost* is more interesting and heroic than his Christ because Satan follows his heart's own devices, whereas Christ is the wimp of God. The confession notices that we construct intentions and modes of action out of our own hearts, and give particular shape to our desires so as to be able to assert something specific. The confession does not condemn this creativity as such, but its use *too much*. "We have followed too much the devices and desires of our own hearts."

The measure, I suppose, is whether the devices and desires of our hearts supplement and fulfill the larger purposes of God the shepherd. Surely this creativity of ours is needed to make the divine purposes specific in our neighborhood and to relate them to our own particular responsibilities. For a person not to construct devices of the person's own heart and to cultivate hearty desires would be to evade personal responsibility. It would be to pretend to be a cipher, wholly moved by some mysterious divine purpose without identity or content. The devices and desires of our own hearts constitute our identity, and it is only through them that we find our salvation. As Christians we are supposed to give ourselves away to the divine life, but we cannot do this unless we have a full self to give away. So of course we should construct and follow the devices and desires of our own heart.

But if we have become lost from the shepherd, if we have lost sight of how our own heart's devices and desires contribute to the larger purpose, then we follow only those devices and desires, and that far too much. If you are musical, cultivate that for the glory of God; but if you disconnect from the glory of God, your music will hypnotize you. If you have a mind

51

and will for business, be productive and make money for the sake of community prosperity and charity; but if you do not set this career within the larger life of God's people, you will be seduced by mammon and always feel hungry. If you love learning or love religion, practice and perfect your skills so that you enrich earth's celebration of the creator; but if you lose sight of the divine immensity within which learning and piety are placed, you will be blinded by the pride of knowledge and holiness, and blindness is worse than the sheep's stupidity.

When we disconnect our hearts from the immensity of God, even by nothing more than innocent stupid straying, the excess in the following of our own devices and desires leads to positive evil. As the confession puts it, we offend against God's holy laws. We move from exaggeration to lying, from selfish hoping to cheating, from competition to oppression, from good fortune to domination, from self-defense to murder. How inexorable it is that we move from stupidity to excess to deliberate, culpable wickedness! Our excuses are at the ready. We didn't mean to do evil; we weren't even aware of what we were doing. But then of course we had to protect ourselves; and if we lost sight of due proportion, it was because there is none other who fights for us, only ourselves. How can we help it if the struggle in the den of wolves, the scramble at the verge of the precipice, or the strangers' war into which we have fallen causes us to do things we ought not do and to avoid things that we ought to do? Who can blame us if we fail to do our obligations or do things we are obligated not to do if that is necessary to protect our safety, our children, our goods, the devices and desires of our own hearts?

Here we have exact measures: lie or lose, cheat or despair, oppress or be oppressed, murder or be killed. We have all here taken our own measures, saying "Go this far and no farther," and then stepping over. We have all pushed the truth then lied, stretched hopes then cheated, struggled then taken unfair advantage, found favor and then gloated, fought in self-defense then crossed the line to aggression that only luck keeps short of murder. Collectively, as a community, we obliterate the measuring line and justify lying, cheating, oppression, domination, and heedless murder as "prudent policy." But individually we know those measuring lines and where we have stepped over. Those lines and our transgression of them measure our identity. More than our birth or our talents or our station or our accomplishments, those lines marking our transgressions measure our identity.

In our hearts we know just who we are, and as the confession puts it, "there is no health in us." The denial of health does not mean that there is no good in us. God finds the worst of us lovely. Each of us embodies and has accomplished many good things. Simply by our birth we reflect the value of our people. And some people are far far better in virtue and accomplishment than others. But no matter how great the quantity or quality of goodness, in every person there are the measuring limits that we have crossed to become liars, cheats, oppressors, bullies, and, in our way, murderers. In this sense there is no health in us; we have found our own measure of righteousness and cross it to sin. Despite our denials of mind and confusions of heart, despite the distractions of false guilts and petty failures used to hide great ones, we know our own measure, we know who we are, and we come to confession praying for forgiveness and restoration.

So the Lenten projectile of finding our measure comes to land in the anxious spooky immensity of the Easter Vigil. In the terrifying suspension between crucifixion and resurrection, where nothing keeps its own shape and God's unmeasured dancing of the mountains and angelic visitations make this tomb-watch a ghost story with much whistling in the dark; the one thing that stands firm, clear, and measured is our sin.

So we rush to the rest of the confession: "But thou, O Lord, have mercy upon us miserable offenders. Spare thou those, O God, who confess their faults. Restore thou those who are penitent; According to thy promises declared unto [us]. In Christ Jesus our Lord." Here we are, Shepherd, find us and bring us home!

So the cruel clarity of sin's measure meets the immensity of God in the promise of resurrection. We wait now, celebrating with the epitomes of Christian things, for the confirmation of new life. But this is not an historical wait. We know what tomorrow will bring. As Paul said, we have already died in our baptism. The baptismal death does not take any of the edges from the measure of ourselves in sin: we are who we are in this regard; and, no matter how much forgiven, redeemed, and sanctified, we shall remain ourselves as sinners. But those measures are no longer the defining limits of our identity. We have also risen with Christ into the divine immensity and glory. We live not for ourselves but for God. We are limited not by the measures of earthly identity but by the degree we can give ourselves over to God's immensity. How do we live in the divine immensity? How do we enjoy resurrection?

I said before that the sheep with the shepherd are either going out to a good pasture or returning home. In this allegory, the good pasture is our life on earth where our measure is taken. Sometimes the good pasture seems like not much; we could have been richer, perhaps, or of different birth, with different talents, and faced by a nicer world. But with the shepherd we can live here, enjoying life to the fullest, doing the work appointed, making a contribution; and even if the way things turn out seems less like a successful career than like a crucifixion, we know that is the model life set for us that leads to resurrection. Going home with the Shepherd, on the other hand, is like the resurrection itself, taking our place in the immensity of divine glory where our cuts, pieces, and sins are surrounded by a fullness that transcends all limits.

But the allegory is false. The way to the pasture is also the way home. We do not first work through crucifixion and then rise to God. God's immensity is not some other pasture than the one we have nor is our pasture outside God's glory. Resurrection does not wait upon Easter. We are not waiting for anything now. For we know and proclaim that Jesus Christ has already died and risen, that we too have died and risen, that the spooky part of the suspension between crucifixion and resurrection is God's own life that dwells in and among us, that God's immensity is terrifying because it gives us unmeasured new life when we were dead to sin's measures, that our ceremonies and songs are not whistlings in the dark but the sounds of the Spirit blowing through the devices and desires of our own hearts, and that we tremble not from fear of God's glory nor from hope for future resurrection but from the travail of the Spirit making us holy now.

Living in God as we do, we must get on with life. Not bound by sin, we are responsible to pursue righteousness in our neighborhood and holiness in our habits. So the prayer of confession ends, "And grant, O most merciful [God], for his sake; That we may hereafter live a godly, righteous, and sober life; To the glory of thy holy Name. Amen."

The Easter Vigil service at Boston University, presided over by the Dean of Marsh Chapel, Robert Watts Thornburg, and the School of Theology's professor of liturgics, Horace T. Allen, Jr., is perhaps the most moving liturgical event of the year; and I have been privileged to be the preacher the last seven years. The service begins with the congregation lighting candles from a fire outside the building and entering the Robinson Chapel in the basement of the Ralph Adams Cram Gothic university church, Marsh Chapel. Like the early Christians in the catacombs, the faithful gather to hear and sing the word, to baptize new catechumens, to celebrate the Eucharist, and finally to listen to St. Chrysostom's sermon for the occasion read in Greek and English. The sermon here was preached at the Easter Vigil in 1993.

7. This Is the Day the Lord Has Made

Read and reflect on Psalm 118:1-2, 21-24; Colossians 3:1-4; John 20:1-18.

I will spare you the jokes about greeting friends you haven't seen here since last Easter. If people come to church only on Easter, this is the festival to pick, not Memorial Day, Mother's Day, or even Christmas. Easter is the day of new life. It points back to the creation of the world and all life; it celebrates now the life, death, and life of Jesus Christ; and it points ahead as the emblem of our constant hope that there is always new life for us. If you come to church on Easter, you hear the word that there is new life for you no matter how trapped, guilty, addicted, habituated to sin, tired, broken, or old. This is the day the Lord has made, and God shall find us in it and give us new life.

I want to call attention to what is special in John's account of the resurrection. Compared with the other evangelists, John uses the account to give his most acute personal characterizations of each of the participants. Mary Magdalene is John's true hero. She arrived at the tomb before daylight to finish the burial rites and found the stone rolled away. Wanting to show someone, she ran back to Peter and John. Those two pillars of the church came to the tomb, misunderstood everything, and went home unchanged. Mary returned, still looking for the body of Jesus to finish the burial, and was confronted by two angels. In the other Gospel accounts, Mary and her companions were terrified at this, fell to the ground and said little or nothing. According to John, Mary was undaunted; she went up to the angels and asked them for the body of Jesus, which was why she was there in the first place. Then Jesus came and Mary, only half turning, thought he was the gardener. So she asked him for the body. He spoke her name, she turned to look, recognized him, and addressed him in the role in which she last knew him: "Teacher." At this point, according to Matthew and Luke, Mary and her friends grabbed Jesus' feet, and he told them to go with the disciples to Galilee. But for John this was resurrection business, and resurrection is but a step on the way to ascension into heaven: Don't get too close because Jesus is different now, not just "teacher." Mary then was commissioned to announce the resurrection and the ascension, which she did as the first official evangelist of the Good News.

Peter and John, by contrast, the first official clergy of the Christian movement, were into foot races. John outran Peter, peeked into the tomb, saw the empty wrappings, and stood back up nonplussed. Peter was slower than John but more impulsive and bullheaded. He pushed right into the tomb and saw that the head cloth had been folded and laid at some distance from the body cloth. Then John came in, and now they both believed Mary that the body was gone. But they still did not understand about resurrection and just went back home. They did not get the point until Mary came later and said, "I have seen the Lord."

What the resurrection means to each of us depends very much on who we are and how we learn. The people like Mary who are full of devotion but won't be swayed from their duty by angels or gardeners are likely to encounter the truth of resurrection and know what to do about it. Speeders like John will get to the right place ahead of everyone else but won't know where they are until someone else tells them. Impulsive blunderers like Peter let nothing stand in their way but cannot see angels and lack the imagination to understand that resurrection means more than an empty tomb. They too need someone else to say the point is not the empty shroud but the new life in Christ.

Just what is this new life? However confusing the accounts about the literal meaning of resurrection, from our standpoint John is surely right about resurrection and ascension, as Luke confirms in the book of Acts: Jesus raised is now at home in God, and we are joined to him now through the Holy Spirit. The kingdom of heaven is here, and we are in it.

In 1993, as it was in the first century, the risen body of Christ that is actual, physical, and historical is us, the church, animated by the mind of Christ as the Holy Spirit brings us more and more into conformity to that mind. As the risen body of Christ we continue in New England and throughout the world the ministry Jesus began in Galilee to bring people to new life. So part of Jesus' new life, and ours too, is the life of the church as the living body of Christ.

But the church cannot be the whole story of resurrection. Think about the lesson from Colossians and its amazing supposition: "So if you have been raised with Christ, seek the things that are above, where Christ is, seated at the right hand of God. Set your minds on things that are above, not on things that are on earth, for you have died, and your life is hidden with Christ in God." The Colossians to whom Paul addressed the letter are dead to their sins by baptism in Christ, raised from the dead in the resurrection of Christ; and they haven't even left town. Furthermore, albeit dead and raised, they still need to be reminded to think on higher things and to give up their bad habits.

Like the Colossians we too, prone to dwell on lower things and still trapped, guilty, addicted, habituated to sin, tired, broken, and old, are right now dead to sin and raised with Christ. This is not a promise for after we die and are shrouded—who can speak of that? It is the presumption of Christians in this life because of what God did in Jesus' life, death, and resurrection.

What does it mean to say we are now raised? Does it feel to you as if we now are enjoying the resurrection of God? Especially when holiness is a task that remains so unfinished for most of us? I apologize for the theological question, but it is the most important question of Easter, and its answer is the most important Christian proclamation.

To get the point of resurrection requires first that we understand where we are in ordinary life and death. It seems to us as if where we are is a great accident. It seems to us as if we are born arbitrarily, on one date when it could have been others, to one set of parents when it could have been others, in one country, of one race, of one gender, of one class, with one palette of talents, with one array of life opportunities, and with one random sequence of chance encounters, all of which could have been otherwise. We are who we are with no reason, and we will die a singular death that could always have been otherwise, a day earlier or a day later, for some other reason. True enough, to the ordinary view of life and death, we are thrown into the world and then out of it like pure chance.

But where we really are is at the flash point of God's creation: without the flash there would be nothing, and with the flash there is us. God creates us on just our birthday, with our parents and no others, in our country, of our race, with our gender, with our class, with our talents, with just our opportunities, and with just our encounters with others. Who we are, with exactly this accidental life, is lovely to the creator. Our lives are defined by the accidents of birth and circumstances, and in this sense we are thoroughly in the world and in no place else. But in another sense, though in it we are not of the world but of God, God's creatures, the products of God's creative act, part of the way God glories forth, tiny pieces in the immensity of God's glory, but crucial pieces; for without us God's glory would be different. Although we make our way here on earth, our home all the time, whether we know it or not, is in the infinity of God's own immense life. For we are the flash point of God's creation.

Think of it another way. It seems that all we are is present here on April 11, 1993. Our past is gone. Some of our past we are glad to get over, of course. Thank goodness people forget. Other parts of our past we would like to relive, but cannot except in memory. The future tantalizes and torments, but it is not yet. All we have is the present, to the ordinary way of looking at things.

But the truth of the matter is that we live in eternity. In God's immense creation we temporal creatures are created to live day by day, beginning with our birthday and ending with the day of our death. This means that somewhere in God's eternal creation every one of our days is future. Somewhere in God every one of our days is present like today. And somewhere every one of our days is past. God does not live day by day as we do but in eternity and holds together all our days as future, all our days as present, and all our days as past. Although only today is present to us, the pulse of the divine life is all eternity. Our minds boggle to think about the eternity and immensity of God, not limited to time or place. Praise God!

The truth about our ordinary life and death is that, although we live only one day at a time, as befitting our temporal nature, our real identity is who we are in God's eternity. Who we really are is how all our dates add up in eternity. We find our true being as eternally alive in God, not only temporally alive in our day-to-day sequence of present moments. So now, in a more profound sense we are in the world but of God. We are in time but of eternity.

Resurrection does not mean simply that we have our true home in God's immensity and eternity. That is our home, raised or not. Eternal life is not the goal; that is where we abide. Resurrection is something more, and here is the issue of new life. Resurrection is the corrective to death of the spirit.

The spirit dies three ways. First of all the spirit dies when it adopts the ordinary view of life that the accidents of our present time are all we are. The ordinary view represents us as by ourselves, without God, apart from God's creativity, unloved in our details. The ordinary view makes it seem that, because God is not one more part of our world, we are not within the divine life.

The second way of spiritual death begins when we notice that the life we have is full of pain, is fragmented so that nothing really adds up or works out, and is too short. Jesus himself is the paradigm. He healed people, most of whom were not grateful; he preached to crowds that were fickle; he taught disciples who nearly always missed the point; he was falsely accused of sedition and executed in the most humiliating way possible, dying too early. Most of us do not suffer that much pain and humiliation; but for some of us it is even worse, and the spirit dies if we then go on to resent life.

The third way the spirit dies is when we realize that we are living as if we were not beloved creatures of God, when we get defensive and reject God's creative love, and when we choose then the life of sin. Of course we know deep down that we are guilty, and then we hang ourselves on the cross. The cross is our symbol of death in profound ways. It symbolizes the way we think of ourselves as abandoned by God. It symbolizes the pain, fragmentation, unfinishedness, and brevity of life. And it symbolizes our own self-punishment. Crucifixion symbolizes all that is wrong with our world, including our own self-enslavement.

But only by facing crucifixion squarely can we see the point of resurrection. We always live in God's eternity but crucify ourselves and one another when we forget that fact. We build a world that represents itself as alienated from God, as merely temporal and not eternal; and then we act as if that were the whole truth. We become enslaved to this way of thinking and are spiritually dead.

From this death we cannot raise ourselves. But the Good News is that God comes to give new life. Jesus was God's bearer of new life who came preaching the kingdom, the right way of understanding ourselves as dwelling in the divine life. Jesus said that, however alienated we might be from the Creator, he and the Father are one, and that he Jesus could be in us. Like us at our best, Jesus tried to do well by God's kingdom but was frustrated in his efforts, misunderstood, falsely accused, tortured, and put to death before his career had hardly begun. The cross was no mere symbol for Jesus. It was the very meaning of his life and symbolic of our lives.

But the short painful life of crucifixion is precisely the death over which resurrection triumphs. When Jesus rose from the grave, he demonstrated that we are not alienated from God; that we live eternally in God's immense creative glory; that sin has no power to enslave us; that we are beloved creatures no matter how wretched we are, no matter how trapped, guilty, addicted, habituated to sin, tired, broken, or old. Jesus' resurrection brings us home to God whom we cannot have left even if we thought to, home to God who creates and loves us even if we reject the Creator, home to God whose immensity absorbs every bit of negativity and resentment we can conjure, home to God whose eternity places our few years in a divine life beyond imagining, home to God whose infinite creative energy lies awaiting our hand if we will but seize that new life.

We Christians indeed died to spiritual death when we were baptized, and we rose with Christ to new life when we accepted that his way of the cross leads home to God. Like the Colossians we know that we are indeed dead and raised again, hidden with Christ in God. Sometimes we need to be reminded of what we know, which is the point of Easter celebrations each year. But we know it. Therefore, for however many decades of temporal life we have left, or years, or days, or hours, let us live them with the loving passion of new life in Christ. Let us bring justice and prosperity to our neighborhood; or if we have too little time or means for that, let us daily amend our habits of sin; or if we have too little time or means for that, let us praise God and sing a song of thanksgiving. For we are not dead but fully alive with the pulse of God's immense and eternal glory. Do you not feel that? This is what resurrection feels like. God has come, entered our spiritual death, gone through it and won, and has brought us back home where God's faithfulness has kept us all the while. Smile about your resurrection now. Sing a song. Like Mary, go tell others that you have seen the Lord this Easter Day. For this is the day the Lord has made. Let us rejoice and be glad in it! Amen.

This Easter sermon was preached on April 11, 1993, the day after the previous sermon, at the Parkway United Methodist Church in Milton, Massachusetts, where Birchfield Aymer is pastor. This is where my wife and I attend when not traveling elsewhere.

8. Deep River and the Wedding Dance

Read and reflect on Exodus 32:1-14; Psalm 106:1-6, 19-23;
Philippians 4:1-9; Matthew 22:1-14.
Anthem: "Deep River" (spiritual); closing hymn, "Lord of the Dance," 261

I am grateful for this opportunity to preach from the pulpit of Marsh Chapel. Last year at the same time I enjoyed a similar opportunity; and the occasion, as some of you know, is that this is the birthday week of Dean Robert Thornburg, the University Chaplain whose pulpit this is; and today he is celebrating with his twin brother, Richard.

Last year the lectionary arranged it so that I could deal with the lead-in material to the texts on divine wrath and judgment, leaving the hard part for Preacher Thornburg on his return. This year the hard texts come today, and I am not disappointed. For it is impossible to preach the good news of the Christian gospel without acknowledging first the depths of where we are. Know it or not, we are launched over a deep river, beating toward the shores of the campground. This is a religious matter, a matter of the spirit. It is more than moral, more than psychological, more than political, more than family prosperity, more than personal fulfillment, more than getting by, more than survival, more than everlasting life. This is a matter of God's vast holiness, its unmeasured power, and what it does to us. What it does is measure our folly and call us out over the deep. God's holiness calls us out over the abyss of the deep river where the fragile rafts of our structured lives are as nothing to the wild winds, waves, and downward pulls. The texts from Exodus and Matthew fairly rattle in their shaky attempts to represent God's terrifying holiness in terms of the human story.

Consider the Exodus story of the golden calf. It is, of course, a story of taking and betraying responsibility in holy matters. What struck me reading it and the surrounding material this time is the lame effort of the author to soften matters with humor. So at the beginning of the text for today, when Moses was delayed on the mountain, the people said, "as for this Moses, the man who brought us up out of the land of Egypt, we do not know what has become of him." Moses was blamed for both leading them into the desert and being inattentive, as if they had no responsibility themselves. Up on the mountain Moses got it from the other side. "The LORD said to Moses, 'Go down at once! Your people, whom you brought up out of the land of Egypt, have acted perversely.'" As if the burning bush, the plagues, the Red Sea passage, and the pillars of fire and cloud were all Moses' doing. Moses quickly passed the people back to God saying, "O LORD, why does your wrath burn hot against your people, whom you brought out of the land of Egypt with great power and with a mighty hand?"

Back in the camp, Aaron, the Super Wimp, assumed that if his brother was gone, so was God; he acceded to the wishes of the people for a home-made god and created the golden calf. The text is clear that he made the calf himself, either with a mold for molten gold or with a shaping instrument—the Hebrew allows both readings. Yet later, in a passage after the text for today (Exodus 32:24), when Moses confronted Aaron, Aaron said, "I threw [the gold jewelry] into the fire, and out came this calf!"

Poor Aaron should have known more about fire, for it marks the unlimited holiness of God. He missed the encounter with God in the burning bush. But he was at Sinai when Moses first went up, according to Exodus 19, when the people were warned not to touch the mountain, the Lord descended in fire, smoke shrouded the mountain like a kiln, the mountain shook and sounded like a trumpet louder and louder, and the people could not come close or the Lord would "break out against them." God is always on the verge of breaking out of the constrictions of a finite meeting to consume those who get too close.

Now Moses succeeded in rebottling God's wrath about the golden calf by saying the Egyptians would make fun of a liberating God who consumed his own people and by reminding God of the promises to Abraham, Isaac, and Jacob. That is, Moses argued that if God is indeed going to enter finite history and care for particular people, there will have to be a deliberate self-delimitation of the divine. The outcome of the golden calf story, which is told in the next chapter (Exodus 33), is that God sends the people of Israel on to the promised land guarded by an angel but without his own presence as up to then. "Go up to a land flowing with milk and honey; but I will not go up among you, or I would consume you on the way, for you are a stiff-necked people" (Exodus 33:3).

We have tended to draw only half the inferences from this story. We have noted that God's wrath is negotiable and that with domesticated substitutes we can be led to the promised land. From this many have gone on to infer that God's wrath is a psychologically harmful fiction and that God's goodness without wrath will build up ego strength and lead to self-fulfillment. We hang on the anthropomorphic conversation between Moses and God and approach God as a friendly interlocutor with whom to bargain for prosperity and justice. And in this we define ourselves as dependent children whose God is equal parts parent and therapist. The specifically Christian version of this is all those faint Christologies for which Jesus is a distant and domestic substitute for the Holy God. The Arians in the fourth century and the Unitarians in the nineteenth wanted not the Holy God in Jesus but a safe angel, an enlightened, human, non-scary, moral guide.

But a half-truth is a dangerous falsehood. For, the Holy God who talks to us does so out of fire and smoke, and we are in constant danger that God will break out against us. The presence of the infinite God to a finite folk is a terrifying miracle. Finite things tend to burst when God indwells, and God scarce remembers to fit. The depth of God's holy fire is infinite. God's saving grace, God's boundless love, God's forgiving mercies mean nothing important unless we receive them from the fiery abyss over which we are suspended in our foolishness and evasions as from a spider's thread.

But fiery abyss and deep river are the same, fire and water, both names of God. And we are being carried across by God's holiness, scary as that is. For Christians the raft across the Jordan is Jesus, and we need to attend to his parable.

Jesus' metaphor for holiness is the wedding feast, with its eating, drinking, and dancing. Those who have been to Jewish weddings know how important the dancing is as the dancers carry the bride and groom around the symbolic circle of life, fertility, and death. Many things are going on in Jesus' parable. The king is like God, his son is like the Christ, and no bride is mentioned. But the guests are called to participate in the wedding, these people whose tradition is this king's kingdom. They have become jaded and go about business as usual, resorting to violence to silence the call from the king. So the king makes his invitation universal; here is an oblique reference to the fact that the people of Israel, from whom Jesus took his identity and the symbols of his teachings, largely rejected him; and his gospel then became directed to Gentiles. But one of the strangers called still does not get the point of the royal wedding and is cast into the outer darkness.

Notice that Jesus' king does not negotiate, as Yahweh did on Sinai. Jesus' parable is resolutely uncompromising. What is arresting about the story is not merely that God extends salvation universally, although Christians have tended to congratulate themselves on that and use it as a subtle gesture of anti-Semitism. What is arresting is the seriousness of the wedding feast, the seriousness of salvation. Here is the New Testament's most famous symbol for the torments of hell—weeping and gnashing of teeth—applied not to some ax-murderer, drug-dealer, or embezzling banker but to a poor schlub who did not dress right. When confronted, he did not lie like Aaron or beg forgiveness but stood speechless; he did not know what he did wrong and probably never knew what happened to him or why. This is not right ritual, not just deserts, not empathic suffering. This is the religious substance of the Spirit. Jesus is tougher than Moses. His parable is painful to people whose God is the tame angel.

Jesus says come to the feast; it is your very being. Do not go about business as usual; your spirit is at stake. Do not destroy those who call you, for there is no life without the feast. Do not blunder to the wedding without the right garment, for you are about to meet your God. Do not fail to be attentive because all else is outer darkness with weeping and gnashing of teeth. The king of the banquet is the Holy One of Israel before whom foolishness is a disaster and whose celebration is the joy of heaven.

How hard this parable is for us, how terrifying, how despairing! For we are nothing if not foolish, unfit, unready, wrongly dressed, distracted, busy, evasive, sinful, wicked, mean-hearted, sucking after golden calves, and on good days cheerfully searching out tame angels. How can we stand before the Holiness that deigns to contract itself in life and smoke, shaking the foundations of mountains with the sound of ever louder trumpets? One whiff of that smoke and our knees turn to reeds, we cry out for domesticated gods, or, which is the same thing, we despair.

Now the Good News makes sense. God has come to us not only in the temporary transfigurations of mountains with fissured containment of divine power but in the person of Jesus, the preacher of parables. Wholly a man, wholly Holy God, Jesus came to us foolish, sinful, idolatrous people with the invitations to the banquet. The invitations say things like I AM the Holy Fire who loves you in your obsessions, your addictions, your dependencies, your weakness, your hysterias, your flights and evasions. I AM the Deep River who loves you in your pain when you fall ill, break bones, lose your house; are devastated by war, oppressed by want, by madness, by failure; grow old, left behind, and creep to death. I AM the Abyss who loves you when creating and destroying you; spinning you a short time for living; shutting down projects before completion; making vain your works, partial your justice, and time-bound your vision. I AM the Creator who loves you when you cannot come to me; when you cannot stand before me; when you have no strength, nor courage, nor resolution, nor acceptance of the infinite with the finite, nor capacity to put aside the idolatries by which you seek to disguise your fear from yourself.

These invitations of love are not on paper but in persons. First in the person of Jesus and then in the persons of his disciples. They have to be delivered individually on the street corners; and to make them convincing, the bearer often has to suffer greatly to illustrate the love. But these lovers, this Jesus and his band, are not just ordinary lovers with ordinary sufferings. They use ordinary love conveyed to ordinary people to contain the holy presence of God, Creator and Redeemer. What shook Sinai to its foundations with blazes, smoke, and the rumbles of destruction fits neatly into Jesus and those in whom his Spirit dwells. The incarnation means God fits in people as God cannot fit in mountains.

The lesson to be drawn from this is not relief at the meek humble humanity of Jesus, but holy terror at this man who is God inviting us home. Jesus is the scariest man who ever lived, with his awesome invitations to the banquet; and when we finally realize just who he is and how he works in us, "every knee should bend . . . and every tongue confess that Jesus Christ is Lord, to the glory of God the Father" (Philippians 2:10-11).

But of course Jesus does not begin scary. He comes first as friend and healer, storyteller and teacher, advocate and bringer of cheer. He comes as we are prepared to receive him and works with who we are. Only after living with his love for a while does it dawn on us whom we have. Only after we have begun to respond do we see that we have been given an invitation from the Shaker of Mountains, the Divine Fire, the Deep River, the Abyss of creation. And then we are properly afraid.

"The fear of the Lord is the beginning of wisdom." Anyone who claims to have met God's love and is not terrified is either faking, self-deluded, or in for a big surprise. St. Augustine said that the process of holiness is the transformation of fear of God into love of God. Fear of divine holiness is the stuff out of which love for God is made. Love for God that does not rise out of fear is fake. It is rather love of a golden calf or a tame angel or a domestic Jesus. Jesus is wild, untamed, the bridegroom carried on the cosmic dance.

For the feast to which we are called, the love for God to which we are summoned, is Holiness itself. We are invited into the Holy Fire where our obsessions, addictions, dependencies, weakness, hysterias, flights, and evasions will be purged from dross by God's refining fire and turned to virtue. We are invited by the Deep River to abandon the sufferings of our illnesses, broken bones, loss of home, ravages of war, want, madness, failure, aging, abandonment, and death to the grace of God in whose life we are brought home. We are invited by the Abyss to embrace our creation and destruction, our short-life allotment, the frustration of our projects, the vanity of our works, our partial justice, our time-bound vision because our finite life arises from the infinite in whom we live and move and have our being. We are invited to come by the Creator who moves us to do so, to stand before divine holiness despite our foolishness by the one who gives us divine strength, the courage of sanctity, the resolution of Christ's heart, the vision of the finite and infinite together, and the heart to live before God.

We are called to love God with the wildness of Jesus, to dance through the Fire, through the River, through the Abyss, into the Creator. We are called to the wild love that steps to the edge of the everyday dark and throws itself into the light with the confidence of the children of God. We are called to follow the Bridegroom Dancer whose dance gives flesh to the Holy. We are called to dance God's steps that touch Terror and Love and consume us.

There is no more serious holy business than this, and all our other business is transfigured in this feast. To ignore the invitation is to be half-dead and to die, and to come without attention is to meet only the Terror, not the Love. When you stand at the edge and the Light comes up that does not blind but ever brightens, step off into the vastness of the divine Abyss, come through the Fire and Smoke, push out across the Deep River; for your Creator calls you with a Love that receives you wildly and makes you holy. For we have met this love, we have touched its source, and we live to pass it on. "What we have heard, what we have seen with our eyes, what we have looked at and touched with our hands, concerning the word of life"—we declare to you what was from the beginning (1 John 1:1). The God who calls in Love and appears in terrible Holiness, assumes those who risk divinity into divine Love with glory. This is life. This is the gospel. Thanks be to God. Amen.

*Robert Watts Thornburg, the Dean of Marsh Chapel at Boston University, cele-
brates his birthday with his twin brother, Richard, on the second weekend in
October; and I have been delighted to be the guest preacher on these occasions.
"God the Witness," "God and the Wealthy," and "Duty First" are other
Thornburg birthday sermons. "Deep River and the Wedding Dance," preached
in Marsh Chapel on October 10, 1993, may not be a particularly accessible sermon; it interweaves many strands of symbols and calls forth resonances with
biblical texts beyond those in the lectionary. But for me it was the most powerful
sermon of my life: it converted me to a new level of spiritual freedom. Instead of
using these symbols to make a point, I abandoned myself to them to engage God
in them directly. Engagement of the divine, not "communication about the
divine," is the real significance of religious symbols; and because of this sermon
I was led to write a book,* The Truth of Broken Symbols *(Albany: SUNY
Press, 1996) in which I not only quote the sermon but analyze its symbols' inter-
play. Of course, the sermon didn't "convert" me as if from the outside; it itself
was the result of my increasing trusting of myself to the symbolic traditions of
the faith.*

9. From Terror to Love

Read and reflect on Isaiah 40:1-11; Psalm 85:1-2, 8-13;
2 Peter 3:8-15a; Mark 1:1-8.

Of the many themes that unite our four Advent texts, none is more problematic than that of highway engineering. Mark follows Isaiah in saying that the highway for God is to be straight. Isaiah goes so far as to say that mountains should be razed and valleys filled in to make the straight road level. On these lines Paul makes a pregnant remark in the Third Letter to Timothy, almost but not quite anticipating later scholarship. I quote at length:

> The prophecy attributed to Isaiah about highways is an eco-disaster and unworthy of the great prophet. Perhaps the lines were a late interpolation by a general such as Vespasian who wanted to move troops quickly, or by a motorist fixated on the New Jersey Turnpike. Let the author of these interpolated lines be known not as Isaiah but as Second-rate Isaiah. The true Isaiah likes mountains and tells the herald to get up to a high mountain and "say to the cities of Judah, 'Here is your God'!" As Ezekiel saw, when God travels by car, rough places make no difference. The point, dear Timothy, is that the prophets saw God coming. (3 Timothy 4:7-11)

As is customary in his later writings, Paul cuts through metaphoric obscurities to the heart of the matter.

All four lectionary texts agree with Paul that the point is, God is coming. So we Christians celebrate Advent. According to Mark, the God who is coming is Jesus. But he cites Isaiah for whom the God who is coming is the Holy One of Israel. The same is true for the psalmist; and when Peter writes of the coming Day of the Lord, quoting Jesus himself, that reference also is to the Holy One of Israel. Of course, this is Mark's own intent: Jesus is that Holy One.

The starting point of our reflections on Advent makes all the difference. If we begin with baby Jesus, cozy in the manger, surrounded by doting parents, oxen, donkeys, angels, and three professors on a junket, the event can be at best a magic show. But if we begin with the reflection that the Holy One of Israel is coming, the mood is surely different.

Who is the Holy One of Israel? How shall we think about this God? There is no way to measure God's holiness. It breaks all our standards, and, in fact, is known again and again in the confounding of measure. So Peter, for instance, says that "with the Lord one day is like a thousand years, and a thousand years are like one day." Related to the confounding of time is Isaiah's contrast between God's everlasting word and the brevity and quick withering of human life. "Surely the people are grass. The grass withers, the flower fades; but the word of our God will stand forever." Moreover, the brief rise and fall of human life is not a matter of incomplete evolution or insufficiency of divine effort in the face of nothingness, as some modern theologians would urge, but the result of the straightforward action of God: The grass withers, the flower fades, *when the breath of the Lord blows upon it;* surely the people are grass.

Our texts agree in another point about the Holy One of Israel: the divine wrath can, and perhaps should, blow us away. The psalmist pleads: "Restore us again, O God of our salvation, and put away your indignation toward us. Will you be angry with us forever?" Mark cites John the Baptist's preaching of repentance, and we know from the other evangelists that John's preaching was fierce: already the ax is laid to the root of the tree. Peter's letter intensifies all the images of divine wrath in the coming Day of the Lord. Immediately preceding the lectionary text Peter wrote that God had created the heavens by the divine word and had made the earth out of water. Once before, for sin God had purged the world with water. Yet now, not the flood but the fire next time. In blazing apocalyptic, a seeming reference to future destruction is transformed to a more than temporal undoing of the creation, "the heavens will pass away with a loud noise, and the elements will be dissolved with fire, and the earth and everything that is done on it will be disclosed." From the Big Bang's star burst to the earth's entropic dissolution in cosmic smoke, but two things are eternal: God's word that creates it all, and God's judgment in which our lives are disclosed—struggling, passionate, sinful, and short. We, who are little lower than the angels, suffer even heaven's fate: all shall pass away but God's eternal glory.

Now you see the immense pressure behind Isaiah's good news. For what comes down that straight and level highway is the terror of God's glory, the glory of creation and ending, of judgment and wrath: "Then the glory of the Lord shall be revealed and all people shall see it together." And we shall not be consumed. The penalty has been paid. The God of power and might, of judgment and wrath, shall come like a lover of the chastised: "He will feed his flock like a shepherd; he will gather the lambs in his arms, and carry them in his bosom, and gently lead the mother sheep." Confounding measures, breaking boundaries! The Holy One of Israel is too far to be imagined and too close to be touched without harm and yet holds us struggling, passionate, sinful, short-lived people like a mother her babies. Glory be!

Where are *we* in all this apocalyptic stretching to acknowledge the Holy One of Israel? After all, this is at least the 1993rd Advent; and as Professor Sampley has reminded us, we are still living between the times.[1] Peter has a clue about where we are when he says that in the new heaven and earth, which lies behind the destruction of all this time and place, righteousness will be at home. So for us, here and now, righteousness is not at home. It is both imperfect and ambiguous. We make the best of a bad lot and are unsure to the end whether, with the best will in the world, we have found the path of least harm. And in our heart of hearts is the constant temptation to steal the pears for the hell of it.

Now comes Jesus to show us where true home is, where righteousness is at home. Home is not some high heaven with bodiless angels apart from the material reality of this world. Nor is home in some glorious past with long-lived patriarchs chatting with God in the garden rather than our present time when God seems silent and distant. Nor is home in some literal distant apocalyptic future where life will be easy, rather than our own time here, with our work and sufferings, our unique problems and historical resources. No, Jesus was born in a stable at the time of the census, they say, lived during the Roman occupation of Palestine, gathered disciples from the social classes available to him, defined a ministry in local terms, and was at home in his time.

On the other hand, the home Jesus showed us is not entirely in his time or ours. His righteousness, like ours, was more powerful in preaching than in performance; perhaps sinless himself, if we believe the claims, he still led others to sin, and brought a sword between generations in families. As a teacher he was less fortunate than the faculty here in quality of students. His healing did not match modern medicine and we know the limitations of that. His movement was as fickle as our work seems vain. He died young, executed in a political accident with no real relevance to his teaching. His righteousness was no more at home in this world than ours.

Yet Jesus was at home. Where? We all know the answer. Jesus was at home wherever he was because wherever he was he found the Holy One of Israel. Jesus lived constantly on the boundary between the finite and the infinite that confounds all boundaries. His prayers addressed the Father above and found the blazing glory within. He taught his disciples to work for a while but frequently to retreat to the mountains to pray. Mountaintop prayers are transfiguring; finite measures are broken and a greater glory breaks forth. But Jesus also found God in sick people, in faithless and weak people, in sinners and whores and embezzlers like us. When people like us are lost, lonely, weak, deluded, addicted, sick, old, despairing, abandoned, beaten, hungry, vulgar, rude, proud, evasive, ugly, infectious, disgusting, and dead in self-pity, Jesus looks at us and sees the Holy One of Israel. He is not repulsed but says, Lo, you are on the highway where God's glory is passing through.

Jesus' ministries of teaching and healing were consequences of his true work, which was leading people home to God. Home is the conjunction between God and our place. Home is the connection that makes the infinite God accessible in the people and problems of our time. Home is the passage from our time to God's time any time. Home is being blinded by God's holy light and seeing everything here clearly. Home is anywhere we might be because God creates there too. "If I take the wings of the morning and settle at the farthest limits of the sea, even there your hand shall lead me, and your right hand shall hold me fast" (Psalm 139:9-10). Jesus leads us to the Holy One of Israel who is everywhere and wakes us up. Jesus is the shaman traveling back and forth across the abyss between finite and infinite. Jesus is the true vine, the original tree of the world rooted in God and whose branches we are. Jesus is the boatman who takes our ship through the storm. Jesus says, "I and the Father are One" and we can go to God through Jesus.

How does he do this? Jesus teaches us to pray and to feed the hungry. He teaches us to pray and to comfort those who are afflicted and in distress. He teaches us to pray and to pursue justice and practice mercy. He teaches us to pray and lead others to God. He teaches us to pray and all else follows that makes for salvation. What is most important in Jesus, his authority, his wisdom, his mission, his commands, his charisma, all come from his instant relation with the Father, the glorious God of creation. Jesus is nothing if not the one who brings God to us and us to God, that meeting which is our home.

But wait. Although this is an expression of the gospel, it is curiously empty, a metaphysical matter of finite and infinite, separation and connection. There is a deeper truth in the Advent proclaimed by Isaiah and enacted by Jesus. I used to think that the deeper truth is the miraculous mercy of God's love. After all, the God to whom the secrets of all hearts are disclosed would be just to be wrathful but instead forgives, loves, and heals. That love is manifest at the foundations in the very creating of the cosmos. Ours is not only a universe of expanding gases but a lovely universe in which everything is good on its own terms. There is nothing we can ruin that God cannot redeem. There is no one so wretched who cannot be given comfort and a share in the divine life. Advent season is one more occasion on which we are opened to the amazing grace of God's love that will not let us go. But I have come to think that God's love is not the deepest truth of Advent.

A deeper truth is that we can come to love God and in that find our salvation. I don't mean merely that we are thankful to God for the good things of life, even for God's saving love of us. I don't mean merely that we can love God in a personal way, as we love a friend, or a Lord. I mean rather that we can love the God of glory, the Holy One of Israel. This seems impossible. For the only possible response to the Mighty One who makes mountains skip like lambs on the hillside, to the Judge who sees all and whose doom is wrath, to the creator in whose universe we are a brief episode of congealed gases, is terror. Stand back from the Lord and fall down, for everywhere is holy ground. Can this terror be changed to love?

By the Advent of Christ, yes. Jesus' commandments are to love God with all our heart, soul, mind, and strength, and our neighbors as ourselves (Matthew 22:34-40). The love of neighbors follows from the love of God, as its image. The challenge in the commandment is to our heart, soul, mind, and strength to love God; and the way to fulfill the commandment is to follow Jesus. To be a disciple of Jesus is to follow him in ministry, extending his Galilean ministry to our time and place. It is to follow him in prayer as he takes us to God's infinite glory. It is to follow Jesus the shaman who goes back and forth from death to life. It is to follow Jesus the true vine onto whose rootedness in God we can be grafted. It is to follow

Jesus the boatman who guides our suffering lives to harbor. The end of all these journeys and joinings is that we come to love the God who is beyond love. The God of terror becomes lovely.

My favorite image of Jesus is as Lord of the Dance. Leading a line of dancers, among whom we are, Jesus dances us through learning and teaching, through serving and healing, through families and friendship, through joys and suffering, from the beginning to life's end, always dancing on deep water, always dancing through the abyss between finite and infinite, always cycling through life and death, dancing a home between God and here, always leaping by grace into God's ever-rising light that does not blind, dancing with earth's rhythms, dancing in armies' clashes, dancing through justice and evil, dancing through joy and pain, dancing through whirling planets, dancing down rivers of hot gases, dancing our time and place into God's glory. Jesus the Dancer leads us into God's glory where we smile, say Amen, and love God, terrible creator, merciful redeemer, home of the dance, our lover, our beloved.

Come, Lord Jesus, and dance us into the new heaven and earth where righteousness is at home, the righteousness of loving God with heart, mind, soul, and strength, from which all else follows that makes for salvation. Amen.

This Advent sermon was preached for the School of Theology chapel service on December 2, 1993. It was intended in my own mind to balance the fierce holiness of God, to which the previous sermon witnessed, with the love of God. Its theme comes from the remark of Augustine's, cited in the previous sermon, that the Christian life begins in fear of God and moves to love. Because the congregation was the School of Theology crowd, I felt free to preach from 3 Timothy as well as from the lectionary readings.

1. Our New Testament professor, J. Paul Sampley, had recently published a book, *Walking Between the Times: Paul's Moral Reasoning* (Minneapolis: Fortress, 1991).

10. GOD THE WITNESS

Read and reflect on Micah 1:2, 2:1-10; 2 Timothy 2:8-15;
Luke 17:11-19

Surely God's mercy is shown in the placement of the harshest words of
divine judgment in biblical books so short we hardly ever find them.
Micah, Joel, Obadiah, Nahum, Habakkuk, Zephaniah, and even 2
Timothy are called to our attention only by the lectionary, and pity to you
if ever you are required quickly to find a passage at a public meeting; if
you have an onion skin Bible whose pages stick together, your situation is
hopeless.

The judgment of God, however, is necessary to hear before the message of
love and mercy makes sense. To be sure, we cannot inwardly *believe* the message of judgment until we encounter divine love. Yet we cannot *understand*
God's love until we have accepted divine judgment. So long as our personal
self-condemnation exceeds that for which we believe God judges us, divine
love and mercy are opaque to us and ineffectual in renewing our lives.

Divine judgment is an unpopular topic, however. Because I am only a
guest preacher, I am going to leave judgment to Dean Thornburg and
take the easy way out by discussing the preparatory topic of divine witness.
Micah wrote, "Hear, you peoples, all of you; listen, O earth, and all that is
in it; and let the Lord GOD be a witness against you, the Lord from his holy
temple." This passage, and the conception of divine witness it illustrates,
is easy to reject in this modern day; for it depicts God as a heavenly voyeur
peeking out from the temple at our affairs. Even more sophisticated interpretations of God as a super fatherly being in some metaphorical sense
who watches us from the outside are easy to reject because they suppose
that God has some kind of personal subjectivity, a private divine con-

sciousness. If God has a personal subjectivity, then it is limited and stopped when it encounters *our* subjectivity. That is what personal subjectivity means: to look out onto a world that is a bunch of objects; when one of those objects is another person looking back at us, we suddenly encounter another personal subject behind those eyes. The world is no longer merely objects but includes some other subjects as well, other people who are mysterious to us, who are as private behind what they do not reveal as we discover ourselves to be private when we are misunderstood. We discover our own depths as we see signs of unrevealed depths in others. If our world contains only objects, no subjects, we never know that there is more to us ourselves than that of which we are self-conscious. Because we encounter other subjects, we can encounter ourselves as subjects and find signs for what lies behind consciousness.

Here is the rub for judgment and witness: behind the presentation of our personal subjectivity lies the heart we don't want seen, the heart we cover up to ourselves except for telltale traces. Now if God is another personal subjectivity, then we are safe! If God has to look out from a private divine standpoint, then we can hide, even better than we can hide from ourselves. When our theology depicts God as a super personal consciousness, then we can play the infinitely postponing game of hide and seek. We hide from God's judgment while seeking God's love. But if by chance we find God's love, it cannot count because it does not address what we have to hide. God cannot forgive us what would be opaque to a divine consciousness, and we live in infinite guilt that God's love is wasted because neither God nor we ourselves have access to that in us for which mercy is needed. If God is a personal subject, we can deceive God as we deceive ourselves. Divine witness cannot mean this.

Return to Micah's text. "Alas for those who devise wickedness and evil deeds on their beds! When the morning dawns, they perform it, because it is in their power. They covet fields, and seize them; houses, and take them away; they oppress householder and house, people and their inheritance." Planning evil may very well be the stuff of dreams and unconscious motivations. We good people surely never sit around and consciously plan to do something wicked for its own sake. Even if we do have a jealous or vicious thought, we know it is private and unexpressed.

But then how is it that we do evil? By accident? Surely not! To seize a coveted field requires planning and connivance. We may hide the covetousness from ourselves, but organizing the seizure requires discipline and use of law. We may disguise love of oil as love of freedom, but it requires strategic intelligence and diplomacy to defeat an Arab state in the Middle East. We may think racism is only a bad dream, but it takes financial organization and elaborate cooperation to redline a neighborhood's real estate. We may think we do not want power over our family and friends, but it takes enormous wit and energy to play the games of status. We may think we feel for victims; but our national, social, and personal lives are elaborately shaped by the efforts to avoid the victim's lot by adjusting to the powers of oppression. According to Micah, God is witness to the stretch between heart and deed; from heart to deed we go, from deed to heart God sees; the witness is the whole, heart and deed, one piece, who we are.

The first lesson of divine witness is that the things we are, heart and deed, count ultimately. In divine witness there is no hiding, no game of self-revelation on our part, no divine mystery. What we are as a matter of fact is the ultimate witness in divine perfection. The witness is not a representation of ourselves in a separate divine mind but our own very being measured in God. We can deceive ourselves, but we cannot deceive God because our very being, lodged in God, is the judgment on us. If only God were over there, another subject, we could hide and dissemble. But God is the infinite creator in whom we have our being. In God's very being our lives are measured by the plumb lines of justice, piety, faith, hope, and love; and in each case we are found wanting. God's witness is the divine goodness in whose context we are judgment on ourselves.

What we are, from dream to deed, counts ultimately. That is a difficult and baffling truth. Come at it from another angle. Remember Luke's story of Jesus and the ten lepers. It begins by saying that Jesus was on the way to Jerusalem; well, we know what happened to Jesus in Jerusalem, so this must be important. Jesus was between Samaria and Galilee, between a hostile foreign land and his home. The lepers kept their distance, as required by law, and asked for mercy, not for healing. Jesus told them to show themselves to the priests, as if they had already been healed and were seeking ritual certification. With nothing more than that baffling instruction, they left, and on the way were made clean. One of the men, realizing what had happened, turned and praised God with a loud voice. He found Jesus and prostrated himself with thanks. Jesus noted that the others had not returned with thanks, and remarked that only the foreigner had done so. He dismissed the man by telling him that his faith had made him well, not Jesus' miracle but the leper's faith.

There are two witnesses in this story. The first is the lone leper who witnessed that God had healed him. The others presumably noticed only their healing. Oh, what I would give to have that leper as a theology student, someone who notices God in even the things of the most selfish joy! There is not enough in Luke's story to indicate how this man saw God's presence when the others did not. There were no special divine devices or incidents, not even Jesus' magic spittle that he used on other healing occasions. The lepers were just walking down the road with hope because Jesus told them the priests could help. The lone leper saw God in Jesus' command and witnessed to God with praise and thanks.

The other witness was Jesus who, in this story, is immediately identified with God. God witnesses the leper's witness because the leper's witness is ultimately important. It reinforces the ultimate status of the leper as a person of faith. The blindness, the mindlessness of the other nine lepers, is also ultimately important for them. They are truly the ones who miss God even when the divine constitution of the universe is doing something of utmost pragmatic interest to themselves. For every one person who sees God's hand in the crucial events of life, there are nine who are blind. Nine times out of ten each of us misses the important presence of God. Everything in life can be told as a straight secular story without reference to God, even the events where strange healings happen. But the truth of reality is that everything can also be told as an expression of God's grace, and the special times are those when God's presence makes a difference to our faith and happiness. Only the leper who knew how to thank was in touch with reality, and God is witness to that. The divine witness to the heroes who are in touch and live the life of thanks is like the divine witness to our dreams of evil and wicked deeds. The divine witness is the truth of who and what we are.

Paul's second letter to Timothy addresses the question of divine witness from yet another angle, one that focuses the gospel message. He quotes a very early Christian hymn:

> If we have died with him, we will also live with him;
> if we endure, we will also reign with him;
> if we deny him, he will also deny us;
> if we are faithless, he remains faithful—
> for he cannot deny himself.

In the main, Paul's point is much like what we have been thinking, namely, that our truest and most important identity is who we are as standing within the divine measure. That divine witness identifies us. And so Paul identifies us with the connection between death and resurrection in Jesus: dying with him, we shall rise with him. Enduring with him, we shall conquer with him. The reverse also holds: if we deny that life, which we might by escaping crucifixion and caving in to pressure, Christ's resurrection and victory are also denied us, simple as that. Of course, there are many questions about exactly what is entailed in crucifixion and resurrection, endurance and victory; but I want to point to the last phrase of the song: if we are faithless, God remains faithful—for he cannot deny himself. What does this mean, that God is steadfastly faithful? If God were a mere person, however superior to others, of course God could deny any faithful divine nature; in some of the images of God in the scriptures, the divine jealousy does indeed seem to deny the divine faith. But Paul's hymn says that God cannot deny the divine faith that loves us. As the hymn refers to Christ as God, it says that Christ cannot deny his own faithfulness, even when we turn from faith to fear and flee.

Here is the gospel message. God is faithful in love to us creatures whatever the witness. When we dream of evil, God still finds us lovely; and sensing that love, we can face our dreams. When we pursue wickedness not for gain but just because it is possible, God still finds us lovely; and sensing that love, we can abandon our enslavement to the possible. When we covet our neighbor's field, God faithfully finds good in us; and knowing that, we can rest in satisfaction. Where we can seize with impunity, God loves us for the guilty conscience; and knowing that, we can put things aside. When we oppress others, and live in ways that hold them in poverty and hurt, God's mercy is still offered; and seeing that, we can turn to righteousness and begin the small steps to justice and virtue.

In none of this is God's witness denied. We dream deeds of evil, and that is who we are. We let the dreams unfold in reality, and those deeds are who we are. We pursue wickedness not just for gain but merely because it is possible, and that is who we are. We covet our neighbor's field, and we are truly covetous. We seize the holdings of the weak and defenseless, and we are truly the abusers of power. We oppress others with poverty and pain, and the truth is that we are oppressors. These faults are who we are within the divine witness. But God loves us despite all this, finds a loveliness in us we cannot bear to accept, and offers us the power to surmount our sin, to transcend our suffering, to find light through our ignorance, and to return to the harmony of the divine peace.

The gospel was in Micah who said God will again have compassion upon us, tread our iniquities under foot, and cast our sins in the sea. The gospel was in Jesus who was the actuality of God's love transforming sinners into saints. The gospel has been spread and fleshed out in the saints across the globe, the great cloud of witnesses to divine love. Down to us that love has come in parents, friends, pastors, and chance acts of kindness by strangers when we were hungry, naked, or imprisoned. Paul told Timothy to be a worker approved by God, one in whom God witnesses love being passed on.

I ask you to witness the divine love of your life in your life. Be like the lone leper who saw God in a life transformed from rot to joy. Wake up to God's love for you that surrounds and accepts your evil heart and wicked deeds. By the light of God's love you will see more evil than you have ever admitted; but in that merciful light you will see how to overcome it. You can help the weak, not oppress them; rejoice in your neighbor's fortune, not covet it; shun wickedness, not do it; have a heart of love, not evil. I witness to you that God's love gives life where you fear death, joy where you bear guilt, understanding where you feel confusion, triumph where you suffer, and says Amen when you see God in life and give thanks. Come join the saints, I ask you, who accept God's witness and witness to God's love. We have souls to make more lovely, cities to make more just, and a world to sanctify. Amen.

This sermon was preached in Marsh Chapel on October 11, 1992, a year prior to "Deep River and the Wedding Dance."

11. Christian Holiness

Read and reflect on Leviticus 19.

Levitical culture is a strange world to us, to modern Jews as well as Christians. Perhaps nothing is as strange as the sharp, obsessive, almost violent distinction between the living and the dead. The living are holy and the dead are unclean. The principal reason for not eating the blood of animals is that blood is life that cannot be profaned as food. The dead are unclean, and those who touch them need to undergo rituals of cleansing. Leviticus 21 lists those close family members whose corpses Levites are permitted to defile themselves by washing and burying, and it warns against ritual signs of mourning; the same theme appears in Leviticus 10, Deuteronomy 14, and Ezekiel 44. Because the dead are unclean and are so easily ready to contaminate the living, the funeral practices in Levitical culture were to get the dead out of the way and underground as fast as possible.

The rabbinic scholar William Scott Green tells the story of the Jewish man who worked in an office with an African American woman. The woman's mother died, and the Jewish man went to the wake out of respect. The Jewish custom, you know, is to sit shiva with the family of the deceased, but not with the body. At the funeral home he approached the family standing in front of the open casket; and his office friend introduced him to her daughter and son-in-law, to her brother and his family, and then gesturing back said, "And this is my mother." "Don't get up," he blurted, "don't get up!" The last thing a Levitical Jew would want is resuscitation of the dead, a blurring of the line between life and death. There are numerous biblical condemnations of witchcraft, which had to do with contacting the souls of the dead.

This Levitical culture obviously had softened by Jesus' time with the Pharisees' then-heretical belief in the resurrection of the dead; but the Sadducees, who denied the resurrection, were in continuity with the temple-sacrifice tradition of Levitical culture. In the mixed and culturally diverse Judaism of Jesus' time, you can imagine how unnerving, how sacrilegious, how spooky and contrary to the sense of what's right and holy, was Jesus' raising of Lazarus. The risen Christ himself, to a faithful Jew of Levitical culture, was a walking corpse, an inadequately buried dead man. When he asked Thomas to touch his wounds, after walking ghost-fashion into the locked room, ooohh! Of course Jesus did not live in a pure Levitical culture; perhaps no one ever did, although Ezra certainly tried hard to create and enforce such a thing. Perhaps one of the reasons Christianity never took hold in Palestine but did among Diaspora Jews was that the influence of the Levitical culture was stronger at home; and Pharisaic, that is, rabbinic, Judaism, flourished abroad. Contrary to our careless assumption that everyone wants the dead to rise, especially oneself, the Levitical is one of the cultures that wants the dead to stay dead. God is the Lord of the living, and the dead are somehow beyond God's covenant because they are no longer free.

Lest we look on Levitical culture as too bizarre, we should remember that its point was to make the people holy, a notion with which Christians should be at home. In what does holiness consist? To begin with, it looks a lot like morals. Leviticus 19 itself lists the importance of leaving some produce in the field for the poor and for aliens; of not stealing or lying; not defrauding nor delaying payment of wages; not mocking the deaf nor tripping the blind; not judging with partiality toward the poor or rich; not slandering nor profiting from someone's death; not hating in the heart; not failing to correct your neighbor, nor taking vengeance nor holding a grudge; not exploiting slaves nor cheating in business; rising before the aged and showing them deference: holiness consists in loving your neighbor as yourself, and the alien counts as your neighbor. Jesus quoted this passage from Leviticus 19 for the second half of the Great Commandment, and he used the parable of the good Samaritan to illustrate its application to aliens (Luke 10:25-37). In fact, Jesus pivoted the perspective so that the Jews appeared as the aliens to the Samaritan.

There also are holiness commandments that seem simply to be savvy advice. For instance, don't let the sacrificed food go too long or it will spoil; let the orchards get established four years before harvesting them; and so forth. Liberal Christians of the last century used to try similarly to explain all other purity commandments as primitive attempts at healthy and efficient living. I suppose the prohibition against sowing two kinds of grain in one field might be for the sake of simplifying the harvest, but I doubt it. The prohibition is part of the same sentence that prohibits wearing a garment with two materials, such as cotton and wool, or leather and silk, and that also prohibits mating two species of animal so as to get a mule or hybrid. We might think that the prohibitions of a man having sex with a slave owned by or promised to another and of selling your daughter into prostitution are moral counterpressures against a culture that reduces women's rights to men's economic interests. Those prohibitions function that way, of course, and are to be applauded for doing so. But their intent is something different, I think. According to Leviticus, the sexual use of a slave is an offense against God, requiring sacrificial atonement, not an offense against a future husband; the reason prostitution is wrong is not the exploitation of the woman but the fact it leads to the prostitution of the land, the people's heritage from God.

Then there are the pure cultic prohibitions: honor the God of Abraham, Isaac, and Jacob, and no others. No idols. Keep things separate because God says God's people should do that to distinguish them from their profane neighbors. Dietary laws are the most often noticed of these commandments that define Israel by separation and distinction. The chapters immediately before and after 19 are elaborate attempts to distinguish Israel as holy from its neighbors by cultic particularities, especially in the realm of sexual relations. Misconduct in sexual taboos seems as spooky and threatening to the Levitical Jews as trucking with the dead, if not more so. Surely the sexual prohibitions have touched hidden psychic fears in us long after the desire to keep the dead dead has lost its force except in zombie movies.

My own belief is that the morality-like commandments, the savvy observances and the cultic prohibitions of mixing different species and doing unclean things, such as eating the wrong food or food wrongly cooked; touching the dead; getting leprosy; or discharging unintentionally through the sex organs are all part of the same cult, the Levitical cult of how to be holy. In a much later and comparative perspective, we can see that the morality-like elements are common to most of the world's cultures whereas the cleanliness taboos seem unique and arbitrary. But in Levitical culture, the reason to be moral was exactly the same as the reason to be kosher: namely, to be holy. Nowadays we attribute justice to a universal moral imperative and cultic particularities to an ethnic solidarity, treating the former as binding and the latter as quaint. In Levitical culture they were of a piece, each kind of item just as serious for holiness as the next, although offenses within each kind might vary in seriousness.

Christianity says exactly the same thing, although with a different content regarding the cult. The cult for us Christians is to be disciples of Jesus, which means joining into his relation to God; taking on his character of love, wisdom, and justice; and carrying on the ministry he started, but as applied to our own time and places. We are leagued together not as a kinship tribe but as a community of different kinds of people responding to the call to discipleship. The cultural and ethnic diversity of the Christians very early led to setting aside dietary laws and ethnic marks such as circumcision and to replacing them with symbols of Jesus' own life as the cultic focal points for liturgy and devotion. Unlike the Levitical culture's belief that holiness consists in Israel's earnest dedication to the observance of Torah, the early Christians accepted Paul's point that human corruption is so serious as to make that observance impossible and to require not a restoration but a new creation: Not a return to Jerusalem but a New Jerusalem.

Christians followed Jesus the Pharisee in shifting the balance in holiness from observance of the laws to the passions of the heart. Not that Levitical culture or Pharisaical Christianity neglected either the heart or the observances, however the observances differ in content: but Jesus shifted the Christian emphasis to the heart so that the letter of the observance became less important and adaptable to different cultures. Christians followed Jesus the Pharisee also in declaring God to be Lord of the Living and the Dead. Death is to be brought into life and overcome. The living and the dead are not to be separated but joined as a cloud of witnesses. No zombie fears for Christians—the dead are part of the larger life of God's people. Christians celebrate the spooks on Hallowe'en for it is the beginning of All Saints' Day. For Christians sin is so bad it leads to death, but death is taken up in life. For Christians, Jesus is the way to God because he goes through death and comes out to life on the other side. For Christians death is no serious separation because nothing can separate us from the love of God, "for I am convinced that neither death, nor life, . . . nor anything else in all creation, will be able to separate us from the love of God in Christ Jesus our Lord" (Romans 8:38-39).

But for all these differences, Jesus based his life, his ministry, and our salvation on the Levitical passion for holiness. Christian holiness is the pursuit of perfection in the cult of Christian living just as much as Ezra sought to perfect the observance of Torah. Now you might not think this is true. You might think that Christian holiness is merely moral perfection and that the cultic part of attending to the symbols of Jesus is an unimportant matter. This would be because so many in our time have come to accept the Enlightenment theory of sin as merely moral transgression. If sin is doing something immoral, salvation consists in the penalty being paid, and holiness consists in making amends and behaving better afterward. This seductive nonsense gives rise to silly doctrines of atonement according to which Jesus, who is supposedly worth more than all people put together, pays off the devil for our sins and starts us with a clean slate. Jesus knew from ancient Levitical culture that sin is no mere immorality but an offense against holiness that makes us unclean. Uncleanliness is disastrously worse than immorality! Whether an immoral act of murder or a broken taboo of diet or unfaithful discipleship, the fault in sin is its offense to holiness. Holiness was the issue for Levitical culture, it was the issue for Jesus, and it is the issue for us.

Now I have been misleading you by speaking about the human project of holiness, whether of the Levitical or Christian sort. Our holiness is but a response to God's holiness. God's holiness is the only motivation for religion in the first place. Levitical culture saw God's holiness and trembled before it. God's holiness shatters our pictures of the cosmos and our stories of morality. God's holiness burns up priests who approach the sacrifices pragmatically. God's holiness strikes down those who reach reflexively to keep the Ark from falling. God's holiness condemns to outer darkness the sleepers and the unready, the unaware and the selfish. God's holiness sears our lips and sends us on missions beyond our means. God's holiness blinds us with too much light, makes us love what we cannot touch, and lifts us to bliss that transfigures the world.

So what do we do? We seek a cult of faithful response. The Levitical cult framed God's holiness with the symbols of divine creation and covenant, and laid out a way of life of faithful response:

> Speak to all the congregation of the people of Israel and say to them: You shall be holy, for I the LORD your God am holy. You shall each revere your mother and father, and you shall keep my sabbaths: I am the LORD your God. Do not turn to idols or make cast images for yourselves. I am the LORD your God. . . . You shall leave [your gleanings] for the poor and the alien. I am the LORD your God. . . . You shall not swear falsely by

my name, profaning the name of your God: I am the LORD. . . . You shall fear your God: I am the LORD. . . . You shall not profit by the blood of your neighbor: I am the LORD. . . . You shall love your neighbor as yourself: I am the LORD. . . . You shall not eat anything with its blood. You shall not practice augury or witchcraft. You shall not round off the hair on your temples or mar the edges of your beard. You shall not make any gashes in your flesh for the dead or tattoo any marks upon you: I am the LORD. Do not profane your daughter by making her a prostitute. . . . And reverence my sanctuary: I am the LORD. . . . Do not seek [out mediums or wizards] to be defiled by them: I am the LORD. . . . You shall fear your God: I am the LORD. . . . You shall love the alien as yourself . . . I am the LORD your God. . . . You shall keep all my statutes and all my ordinances, and observe them: I am the LORD. (Leviticus 19:2-37)

The Christian cult is no different in being a way of life that attempts a faithful response to God's holiness. What distinguished Jesus was not his teachings, which were part of the Pharisaical movement; not his ministry, which was like others; nor the messianic claims about him, which were made about so many others; but his love of God's holiness. Long before people understood him, they were attracted to Jesus because he so manifestly was able to love the Holy One of Israel. Christians follow Jesus into discipleship to do good, to spread his message, and all that; but far, far more than that, in order to enter into his pattern of holiness. The encounter with God's holiness shakes us into fear, as Leviticus said, which is the beginning of human holiness. But Jesus transformed that fear to love, the perfection of human holiness. Our sins seem to stand in the way, such an offense against God's holiness that we can only pray for death as saving separation. But Jesus calls us to follow the path of loving God and neighbor, to follow through the flood of duties and distractions, to follow to the cross, to cross the river into campground, to follow across death and the abyss, to follow into the light, to follow Jesus' dance from life through death to glory where God's holiness consumes all dross, to come at last to bliss where God is our beloved and all holiness is one.

I invite you, my friends, to turn to your studies, your ministries, your families, and the circumstances of your lives with the delight in which their creator beholds them. Engage them with faith, accepting the struggles, uncertainties, ambiguities, frustrations, failures, and finally their finish. This is your life; you have no other. But please rejoice with me that behind and within it all, however obscured, is the holiness of God. This world is not what it seems when we are half asleep. I have no idea how many cults there are on earth and elsewhere that frame human ways of life responding well to God's holiness. The Levitical is one and the Christian is another. We are invited to follow Jesus in the Christian way to holiness, God's holiness not ours. Our holiness comes when we awaken to God's.

The introductory Hebrew Bible class at the School of Theology approaches its texts with historical and literary methods of analysis. But the point is to under-stand their spiritual significance. Professor Katheryn Pfisterer Darr designed the course to include a sermon by one of the School's preachers every other week, showing how the text under study can be approached by a homiletical exegete. She assigned me Leviticus, probably on the ground that only a dean whose excitement peaks in bureaucratic memoranda would be turned on by lists of rules. The sermon was preached in Robinson Chapel on November 9, 1994.

12. Eternity in Three Mysteries of Time

Read and reflect on Psalm 114, Romans 6:3-11, Luke 24:1-12.

According to the reckoning of Jesus' people, since sundown just past we have been in Easter Day, waiting for the day to unfold. Waiting through the night to sunrise is an uncanny time: like always, time is passing; but what is happening is the unfolding of eternity, not just the passing of time. Time is difficult enough to understand on its own. But it is also the icon of eternity through which we understand God and our salvation. Plato said time is the moving image of eternity. I think rather that time is the static course of markers through which eternity moves as infinite life in finite things. Time is not a moving image: God's fire, and our finite flames of that, are what move; and time is that through which this life moves.

Now these aphoristic statements about time and eternity are a far cry from anything of which the women would have been thinking at the time on Easter eve when, after the enforced rest of sabbath, they rushed to gather the spices to finish embalming their fallen Lord. Rather, I wager they wondered among themselves about the catastrophic ruin of their yearly Passover, because their firstborn son and hope had been slain, an innocent pawn in the distant political game of rulers and revolution. They must have felt like Egyptian mothers and deeply conflicted about at least this part of the yearly cycle of festivals in the cult of the Almighty. I also wager they wondered about what to learn from all this, if anything, about God's alleged destiny for Israel. And they must have wondered, with both doubt and hope, about Jesus' dark references to death and resurrection. These thoughts, not Plato's topic, are the mysteries of time through which

I want us to reflect on eternity while waiting tonight: the time of the liturgical calendar, the time of catechesis or learning, and the time of death and resurrection.

In case you hadn't noticed, the whole idea of the liturgical calendar is a weird mystery. Nearly every religion has a yearly cycle of festivals, often broken down into weekly and sometimes daily and monthly cycles, and sometimes accumulated into multi-year cycles such as the Jewish Jubilee. Christians observe a weekly cycle of worship from Sunday to Sunday; and some churches have weekly prayer meetings, group fellowship, and choir practice. Denominations such as the United Methodist have a monthly eucharistic cycle. Some communities observe a daily cycle of monastic prayers at set times, at least morning and evening prayer. The cycling of worship and festivals, cycles within cycles, shapes the soul's imaginative heart by reenacting in liturgies the symbolic content of faith.

Think of the festivals of the Christian year. Advent means God comes to save the world, culminating in Christmas when that Advent is in the form of a human person. God fits into the likes of us. Epiphany is the manifestation of the indwelling God to the world, beginning with the adoration of the magi in the cave and concluding with the transfiguration of Jesus on the mountain. Lent begins the season of personalized response to God in our midst. Mardi Gras is a fit celebration of the glories of the flesh, to be so graced with divinity; but Ash Wednesday begins the season of repentance and discipline with its double meaning. As works righteousness, Lenten penance culminates in the false triumph of Palm Sunday and the betrayals of the Garden and the Cross. As reception of the Holy Spirit for our own sanctification, Lent takes us through our own petty triumphs and betrayals, and crosses, to the life of resurrection. Good Friday and Easter together mark the Christian understanding of life's real nature: sin, suffering, sickness, too much to do, too little help, incompetent support, uncomprehending colleagues, incomplete projects, bad luck, accidents, violence, death—but also resurrection and glory, forgiveness of sin, surmounting of suffering, healing of sickness, reward for work, abundance of life, sharing with others, passing the light, fulfillment in God, providential blessing, amazing grace, peace, vision, and bliss. Embracing the cross in faith we are transformed into new creations loved by and loving God, all love's excelling. After Easter we receive the blessing and commission of the ascending Christ who shows us the way home, and then with Pentecost we enter the life of the spirit to renew ourselves and our world in the covenant of sanctified life, awaiting the return of our Lord, next Advent.

The point of the liturgical calendar is not merely to teach and remind us of these elements of the Christian faith with enough regularity for them to sink in, although that purpose is served. The point is rather to spread out in time, in a yearly understandable cycle, the celebration of truths that are not sequential but compacted together in eternity. We need only reflect on some of the differences between the Gospels of Luke and John to see that the presentation of the Christian message in drawn-out story form, fit for punctuating a liturgical year, is a rhetorical device, not just a report. Luke, as you know, cites the holy number 40 for the days Jesus spent in the wilderness, after which our Lenten season is modeled. Luke says that 40 days after Easter Jesus ascended into heaven; and then 7 weeks after Easter, like a sabbath, comes Pentecost, the reception of the Spirit on the festival day by which Jews celebrate the reception of the Torah. Luke's narrative is made to order for a liturgical calendar and may, in fact, have been written to reflect an early version of a calendar.

John, by contrast, is noted for his "realized" eschatology, not representing things as drawn out in a leisurely story but compacted as if finite time bursts with the infinite. John does not begin his Gospel with stories of Jesus' parents' relatives, or lists of ancestors, or annunciations, or birth narratives, or holy old saints happy to meet the Messiah, but with the Logos of God suddenly appearing in a blaze of light, identified as Jesus by John the Baptist, and set running to the end. Easter day, for John, begins with resurrection before dawn, and by evening Jesus has met his disciples, given them their commission, and breathed on them with the Holy Spirit—wrapping up the resurrection, ascension blessing, and Pentecost in less than twenty-four hours. John interprets Jesus' subsequent appearances to the disciples as a kind of checking up on the Christian movement. John records no ascension lift-off into the clouds but ends his Gospel with Jesus giving the disciples a symbolic fishing lesson, focusing their minds on love and ministry, and cooking them a hearty breakfast so they can be about his business. I rather like that ending myself. But Luke draws out the resurrection, ascension, and Pentecost into separate festivals, each of which marks a crucial transition from the broken earthly "school of Jesus" to the commissioned church under the authority of the Holy Spirit. For Luke, the whole story is the foundation of the church, and Jesus' biography is told as if a liturgical exemplar.

I want to make two quick points about the temporal spread-out-ness of the liturgical calendar. First, it is a way of representing and celebrating the eternal truth of salvation which is so complex it cannot be said all at once.

That is, Jesus' identity cannot be grasped without the ancient promises and the recognition of their fulfillment in him, so Christmas needs Advent and also Epiphany. The Cross cannot be understood without the resurrection, but then the resurrection cannot be understood without the Cross either. The Pentecost church cannot be understood without the ascension which points toward fulfillment; the ascension cannot be understood without the Pentecostal gift of the Holy Spirit. I say these things lightly, as if the calendar is a big puzzle all of whose parts fit together. In fact, each of these is a mystery much deeper than any story-like set of roles they play with respect to one another. The Lukan story, like the liturgical calendar, does not explain them by its temporal form but only shows that we need to come to terms with them all, regularly, again and again.

The second point about calendar time is the converse: the spiritual state of any one or several of us is always at some one point, perhaps epitomized by a liturgical season. We are in shock that God comes for us, or amazed at how much more God is than we imagined, or bent under a load of penance, or suffering a special cross, or giddy with a sense of new life, or focused in some discipline of holiness, or consumed in a ministry. Entering fully and with faith into that spiritual state, the other states, reflective of other seasons, are pushed to the background, their images and frames subordinated to where we are at the moment. But the eternal truth expressed in the temporal calendar is that we are engaged in all those other states too. Our identity is not confined to our state at the moment but to the whole being of a Christian before God. Though we are not whole at any one time, we are whole in eternity; and the cycle of the liturgical year symbolizes this. Eternal wholeness plays out in time's cycles. So it does not matter much if we have our off days, or if sickness makes us confused, or sorrow makes us angry, or age makes us senile, or dying makes us selfish and self-pitying—faith too has its seasons. Just as the whole of the gospel takes in all the seasons, so does the whole of our redemption and holiness. What we are at any one time is such a tiny fragment of our eternal identity in the presence of the eternal and infinite God.

You will have noticed my blatant shifting of the topic from the coherence of the liturgical year to the fullness of the gospel to the fullness of salvation in our eternal selves. That trajectory of topics is part of the way I mean to point from time to eternity. Let me come at it another way. What is there for a Christian to learn, and when? What is the timing of catechesis? Of Christian education and growth?

Here in this basement, like in a catacomb, we are involved in an ancient rite, filled with symbolism and deep spiritual resonances. I have been talking sophisticated Christian liturgical theology, heavy with imponderable resonances. This is advanced stuff, for people who like to consider themselves the serious faithful. If what I've been saying feels a little over your head, don't worry: it certainly is beyond me. But Christian learning begins at a far simpler level than that of anyone in this room, except perhaps young Petersen. The Great Commission (Matthew 28:18-20) is to take the gospel to all the world; and so long as we are talking in this sophisticated way, we have not reached much of the world. The world is not Christian, not even leftover fake Christian. We have not taken the gospel to the world until we have learned to talk about it in the language of the world. My high liturgical talk sometimes stands in the way of the church's mission because it addresses those already within the fold whose catechetical clock has been running for some while, already at least committed to learning the special Christian language, already in a family that will teach "Jesus" among the first words.

Of course the language of the world might not in its own terms be able to speak the gospel. That secular language, especially its cheap commodified dialects, need to be transformed by engagement with the Christian language in order for the gospel to be expressible. But that's the point: we need to meet and engage those for whom this special biblical and liturgical language is foreign and perhaps alienating.

The issue is not about evangelism per se, but about the process of drawing people into the Christian way and leading them to deeper and deeper meaning. The evangelical moment starts the time of catechesis. There are many models for this. Augustine, for instance, said that a start is made when God is encountered as holy and terrifying; and the catechesis of the Christian life is supposed to turn the fear of God into the love of God. That takes many steps. In our time and since the Reformation, it is common for a start to be made by helping people understand how unhappy and fragmented they are and by offering them the gospel as what they are missing. The early steps on the Christian path take the form of finding what God can do for me; this becomes transformed to steps of doing something for God; and finally the Christian life surmounts both doing and being done for and becomes a song of praise and vision of bliss. The time of catechesis begins with people who think that now is all there is, introduces them to a common history with Jesus, broadens their vision to a cosmos of creation and a world of neighbors, sets their souls to deepening by time's cycle of sacred symbols, and points them to see eternity through the vectors of these learning times.

What this means for each of us personally is that we are somewhere between the beginning and the end of our time of learning. We look back with gratitude and perhaps a little embarrassment to the earlier levels of spiritual formation that we have outgrown, and we worry we might have forgotten something. At the same time we need to be aware of how far we might yet go and how that future in our time of learning might make our present seem as preliminary as our past. At least we can be sure that so long as our time is running, we have more to learn; and in the matter of eternity, whatever we learn through our symbols is always surprising.

The time of resurrection is the greatest surprise. Like Peter in our Gospel lesson, we are left amazed. Whether you follow Luke's or John's version, Jesus' resurrection was not a return to the life he lived before crucifixion. In the lesson from Romans, Paul put the surprise most poignantly. Just as we participate in Jesus' death by being baptized, so we participate in his resurrection and "walk in newness of life." "So you must consider yourselves dead to sin," said Paul, "and alive to God in Christ Jesus." By taking on the life of Christ, which is enacted in baptism, we become dead and alive at once, crucified every day and "raised by the glory of the Father." All this before we die in the ordinary sense. What a mysterious way to think about this waiting time on Easter evening!

The passage read from Romans is part of a longer argument in which Paul is answering the accusation that he encourages loose living by preaching that Christians are free from the law. Paul's response is, Of course not!—so long as we are living we need to work to make sure that sin does not "exercise dominion in [our] mortal bodies" (Romans 6:12). But Christians do not live in merely ordinary time: we live in Christ who is crucified and raised, and thus also in resurrection time. Think, for a moment about how Paul distorts the usual symbols. Baptism in the Gospels had usually symbolized washing people clean from the stain of sin. But for Paul baptism here symbolizes dying and being buried with Jesus in a grave of water. By being baptized we are committed to take on the kind of life Jesus led, which suffers many crosses and leads to death. Paul does not leave this death-by-water as a symbol for suffering and finitude: he says rather that dying kills the body of sin and for this reason death is a gain. Even babies die to gain a life! Of course, in ordinary time we must work constantly to become more holy and not sin. But in resurrection time, the self that would be committed to sin, obsessed by it, and in bondage to it is dead. Therefore, as buried now with Christ and raised now with Christ, we are not in bondage to sin, even in ordinary time, and should get on with life.

But how can we be in ordinary time and resurrection time at once? In ordinary time we have our recalcitrant tasks with sorrows, frustrations, pains, and inadequate help, hoping to make it through to the end without doing much harm. At the same time, in resurrection time we are dead to sin, buried with Jesus in the waters of death, and raised to new life in which we confront not sin but the glory of the Father. How can this be?

This life does not feel to me like being dead to sin—sin is alive in my life—nor do I feel much like a New Being, only at best somewhat refreshed after vacations.

But, of course, how it feels to us in ordinary time is not what counts. What counts is the fact that resurrection time is life in God, life in God's eternal life, life where we join Jesus at God's throne, life around the heavenly banquet table. The scriptures use image after image from ordinary time to point us to eternal resurrection time. God's eternity is like a place to which we go; Jesus goes to prepare a place for us; we are going home. God's eternity is like light that makes everything clear after the darkling plain of ordinary time. God's eternity is like a kingdom in which we are living even though we think we are living in secular chaos with no judge and no redeemer. God's eternity is like coming back to life after ordinary death, but not for more ordinary life. Resurrection time does not just come later; for Paul, it is now. To be buried with Christ in the waters of baptism is to die in the deep of creation, whipped up by the wind of God and formed by the divine word, so as to come out a new creation. Resurrection time cradles ordinary time itself; it is a return to origins. Resurrection time is drawn out by the glory of God that Paul says raises Jesus; it is a consummation in God's glory. Resurrection time joins Alpha to Omega throughout ordinary time.

Resurrection time, you see, is our time in God's perspective, and we glimpse that perspective not in ordinary feeling but in faith. We need the time of the liturgical calendar to shape that faith, to give it nuance and discernment, and to allow its mysterious variety to be run through and gathered up. We need the time of learning, catechesis time, to give faith depth, to learn that all symbols are broken like the static markers of ordinary time and yet the symbols draw us in to what they symbolize. We learn together that Christians do not live in ordinary time alone, but that ordinary time itself is but the manifestation of resurrection time. In resurrection time we are who we really are before God: judged, loved, given new life, made holy, made lovers.

Only through faith now do we catch glimpses of our true time in God. Through baptism we say yes to that time for ourselves and those we love and enter into the way of life that celebrates it. Today is not the Advent festival of God coming to us; it is not the Christmas festival of God incarnate; it is not the Epiphany of redemption, nor the Transfiguration of the finite, nor Lenten penance, nor the Pentecostal commitment to ministry. It is the festival of the celebration of resurrection time, of our life with Christ in God and before God, drawn from ordinary time's deadly bondage by God's glory to new life. Dead and raised in the midst of ordinary life— that's how God sees us, how God creates us, how God redeems us, and how we can love God. Of course we tremble in this uncanny time when the day of resurrection is upon us! Whisper with me the song of resurrection faith:

> Love divine, all loves excelling, joy of heaven, to earth come
>   down;
> fix in us thy humble dwelling; all thy faithful mercies crown!
> Jesus, thou art all compassion, pure, unbounded love thou art;
> visit us with thy salvation; enter every trembling heart.
>
> Come, Almighty to deliver, let us all thy life receive;
> suddenly return and never, nevermore thy temples leave.
> Thee we would be always blessing, serve thee as thy hosts above,
> pray and praise thee without ceasing, glory in thy perfect love.
>
> Finish, then, thy new creation; pure and spotless let us be.
> Let us see thy great salvation perfectly restored in thee;
> changed from glory into glory, till in heaven we take our place,
> till we cast our crowns before thee, lost in wonder, love, and
>   praise.
>
> Charles Wesley, 1747

This was the Easter Vigil sermon in Robinson Chapel on April 15, 1995. At the service, an infant, Caleb Petersen, was baptized and reference to him is made in the sermon.

PART THREE
JESUS CHRIST

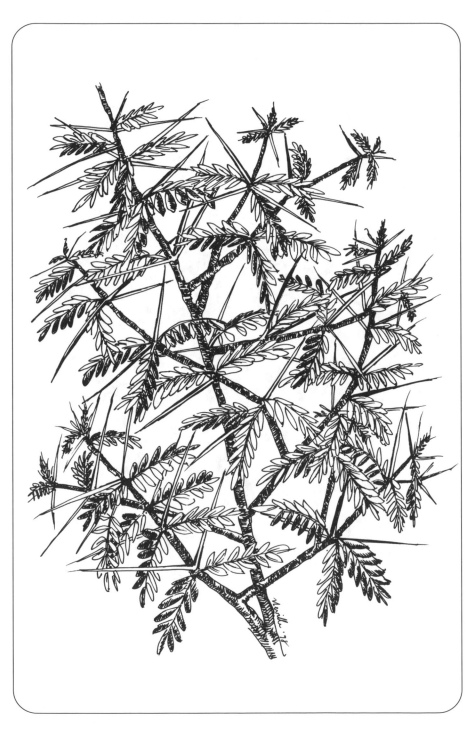

Crown of Thorns

13. FEAR WHAT?

Read and reflect on Mark 16:1-8, Romans 6:3-11, Ezekiel 36:24-28.

The ending of the Gospel of Mark fails to satisfy Christian sensibilities. It records no resurrection appearances of Jesus, only the empty tomb. The two Marys and Salome are filled neither with deep piety nor with resurrection joy, but rather are seized with amazement and terror. The young man in white tells them to proclaim that Jesus has been raised and to direct the disciples to go to Galilee where Jesus will appear to them all. But Mark is explicit: "They said nothing to anyone, for they were afraid." So much for triumphant Easter proclamations.

Mark's Gospel is the earliest, as we know, and the other Gospels were quick to improve upon its resurrection account. In Matthew and John, the risen Christ in person appears to the women at the tomb itself and then to others later. In Luke the women get Peter and John to look into the tomb; and it is the men who are seized with terror, amazement, and incomprehension. The scholars among us will note that these supplements in the other Gospels to Mark's ending demonstrate the existence of revisionary feminism in the church long before Elisabeth Schüssler Fiorenza. Matthew, Luke, and John make the women the first to see the risen Christ, the first to proclaim the resurrection, and the first to convey Christ's orders to the church about where to go; and those post–Markan Gospels represent the men rather than the women as the ones struck dumb with fear. The politics of feminism aside, the whole church thought the revisions a good thing and within a few centuries had added a variety of supplementary endings to Mark's Gospel itself consisting of quotes and paraphrases from Matthew, Luke, and John. Most Bibles list these supplementary endings as a series of appendices to Mark.

Despite its failure to satisfy narrative sensibilities, Mark's original ending was the most powerful and instructive. Amazement and terror. Withdrawal to silence. Full stop. What was so different as to be amazing? What did they fear? Why hold in the breath of speech?

To understand the amazing difference we need to imagine how the disciples would have been regarding their situation up to that point. Jesus first appeared in their midst as one who quickened hope that the ancient promises of Yahweh would be fulfilled. John the Baptist had advertised Jesus as the redeemer promised in Isaiah. Jesus himself spoke of God's promises of redemption, of their own time as the time of fulfillment, and of himself as the Son of Man and Messiah. In Jesus' age the divine promises in the prophets and Torah must have seemed very distant and confused. Because of the Roman occupation, the national identity of Israel was compromised and the existence of a puppet government and a community of temple priests and judges subservient to Rome created only a mirage of religious authority that fooled few if any Jews. Furthermore, three hundred years of Hellenistic culture had made the anthropomorphic imagination of the Torah and the prophets seem quaint and unsophisticated. Although isolated communities wanted to return to the old ways in which the promises made sense, and other wandering preachers claimed to be about to restore Israel politically and spiritually, they were the lunatic fringe.

But the months of traveling with Jesus had given his own group of disciples a renewed sober sense of the heritage of Israel, a new understanding of the promises and how they could be brought up to date. The disciples were taught to reaffirm the past as the ground for present life and to see themselves as heirs of the promises. God's loving care was newly perceived to be in continuity from the creation of the world to the covenants with the patriarchs, the exodus, and the comforts of the prophets, all as rehearsed in our readings from the Word tonight, down to their own time.

Yet Jesus the prophet, Son of Man, Messiah, fulfillment of the promises, the charismatic teacher with authority, had just been killed. Betrayed by one of their own, summarily convicted on false charges by the officials of Caesar and God, speedily crucified with thieves, and rushed to a borrowed grave. The past of divine care on which they had grown their hope was swept away between the supper and sunset of one day. The old past of confused authorities, alienated religion, vain promises, and the childishness of hope was revealed as the reality. When Jesus had extended himself beyond the Galilean hills of personal discourse to Jerusalem's streets of real power, Reality blew away his salvation stories like smoke rings. The truth of the past like the present is sin; the promises are fantasies; and that good man Jesus who stirred their souls, to whom they gave their hearts, who accepted their love and let them be filled as lovers at last, was crushed by the blind inertia of unclean affairs that neither knew him nor cared. Unclean, that's the situation. Unclean, that's how it always was and is. And the best that's to be done with the unclean inertia of an unclean past is to spice the sad body of Jesus to delay decay.

So Mary Magdalene, Mary mother of James, and Salome went to the tomb. Some of us know what that feels like. Even professional Christians such as myself sometimes feel that our work is little more than spicing a dead body to delay decay.

But to discover the tomb empty, to be told by a shining man dressed for baptism that the Lord is *risen*, is to have a revelation of what is truly real and what is illusion. The sorry unclean truth of sin's inertia is not the last word! The promises are not vain! Wisdom and fantasy are reversed! The spices are not needed! No wonder they were amazed!

And we can understand what they feared. For all their time with Jesus and for the brief days of despair without him, the disciples understood themselves through their past, first with hope, then without hope. But with the resurrection the past was transvalued. Jesus is more than prophet, Son of Man, Messiah, or anything else that could be defined by the inertia of the past, even by patriarchal divine promises. The resurrection is the apocalyptic shifting of the orientation of meaning from past to future. If Jesus is raised and waits for us in Galilee, what now? the women asked. What now? What is this uncanny future that lies beyond promises?

I have no idea how fast the women at the tomb thought about this. The mere question is enough for terror. But if they had thought like Paul, they would have seen the future implications of Jesus for themselves. Not just a beloved teacher, the risen Christ is a new kind of reality in which they, like us, must enter. With our baptism, we enter into Christ's death and resurrection. Paul wrote:

> Therefore we have been buried with him by baptism into death, so that, just as Christ was raised from the dead by the glory of the Father, so we too might walk in newness of life. . . . We know that our old self was crucified with him so that the body of sin might be destroyed, and we might no longer be enslaved to sin. (Romans 6:4-6)

Thus part of the terror of the future is that we shall be freed from sin. The comforting thing about sin is that we know who we are in sin, and we know in what we participate. Paul did not say that dying to sin in baptism will prevent us from sinning any more. In this passage as well as others, he said that Christians who already have died and been raised with Christ still need to work on sinning less and disciplining ourselves for perfection. Rather what Paul means is that, in dying to sin, the uncleanness of sin no longer controls us. In sin we participate in the great unclean inertia of the past. We are part of the confusions of authority; of the cycles of decay and renewal of religious purity; of the social forces of poverty, greed, mindlessness, inattentiveness, egoism, neglect, and narcotic stupor. We learn to be unclean when we learn to speak and relate to other persons. But listen to what Ezekiel said: "I will sprinkle clean water upon you, and you shall be clean from all your uncleannesses. . . . A new heart I will give you, and a new spirit I will put within you; and I will remove from your body the heart of stone and give you a heart of flesh" (Ezekiel 36:25-26). This is not to say that things will get better and that God will take care of us but that God will make us different. Heart transplants are terrifying. There is no natural innocence, only holy cleansing.

Rising with Christ is as terrifying as dying with him. Going down into the cleansing water is hard enough. How can we face coming up clean? This is the terror of the future. We do not know the ways of cleanliness. And we do know that the old inertia of the world is still with us. Like Jesus we will be beaten in history's way. There is no resurrection without crucifixion, no cleanliness without the drowning death that cleanses. But by what word shall we live as crucified and risen with Christ, dead to sin yet still sinning, cleansed from sin but incarnate in an unclean world?

The terrifying answer, surely glimpsed by the two Marys and Salome at the tomb, is that our recourse is only to follow Jesus as best we might and leave the rest to God. Without God's spirit, even the risen Christ is dead to us, mere teacher and beloved leader, long gone. With God's spirit, resurrection accompanies crucifixion. John's Gospel (20:22) reports Jesus breathing on the disciples after the resurrection as if to ordain them, saying, "Receive the Holy Spirit." You know the words for breath and spirit are the same—in Hebrew, Greek, and Latin—and the passage might just as well mean "Jesus inspired them and said 'receive the Holy Spirit' " or "Jesus breathed on them and said 'receive the holy breath.' " Either way, the word carries both meanings together, and always has. The first sentence of Genesis means both that the spirit of God swept over the waters of chaos and also that the wind of God swept over. Wind or breath is the symbol of God's spirit, and we must wait for that wind for remaking. But too often that leaves us sitting together in some upper room wondering what to do next. The inertial promises of the past are insufficient to make new people of us. The past has lost its mooring. We also need the breath of God, the divine spirit. We cannot be raised with Jesus until Pentecost. Amazed at the new life of Jesus into which they were called, the women at the tomb were terrified about what it might mean, without the Holy Spirit.

Think again of Mark's text. The women were not only amazed and afraid but also struck dumb. They were told what to say, but for fear could not say it. Beyond cleansing water and divine wind we need God's word for life. In Genesis there was no creation with just the chaotic waters whipped up by the windy spirit. Creation waited upon the word that said, Let there be light. Listen to Ezekiel's equivalent:

> [God] said to me, "Mortal, can these bones live?" I answered, "O Lord
> GOD, you know." Then he said to me, "Prophesy to these bones, and say
> to them: O dry bones, hear the word of the LORD. . . . So I prophesied as
> I had been commanded; and as I prophesied, suddenly there was a
> noise, a rattling, and the bones came together, bone to its bone. I
> looked, and there were sinews on them, and flesh had come upon them,
> and skin had covered them, but there was no breath in them. Then he
> said to me, "Prophesy to the breath, prophesy, mortal, and say to the
> breath: Thus says the Lord GOD: Come from the four winds, O breath,
> and breathe upon these slain, that they may live." I prophesied as he
> commanded me, and the breath came into them, and they lived, and
> stood on their feet, a vast multitude. (Ezekiel 37:3-10)

The winds were summoned by the word to give life breath. Nothing happened to bring Ezekiel's bones to life without the word of prophecy. Only the word can turn water and wind to new life. The word turns amazing novelty and fearsome spirit into a determinate direction: Go to Galilee.

Distinct as they are, spirit and word are closely related. The word needs the spirit to confirm it just as the spirit needs the word to give it direction. The two Marys and Salome refused to speak the word they had been told because of their fear, and the fear was the terror of the future without the spirit.

So we tonight are very much like those women at the tomb. We come weary with the nagging fear that our lives are only the applications of spice to delay decay, nostalgic for lost hope. We are therefore astounded to encounter in this room now, again, the living presence of two millennia of the risen body of Christ, proclaiming the word in Scripture and song, passing down the quickening spirit from Jerusalem to Boston, and preparing to commemorate our own baptism into death to sin and new life in Christ. Here we are, the real and vital Christ. Like the shining young man in the baptismal gown, we are filled with joy and may be excused if we gloat on the gospel a bit. But like Mary, Mary, and Salome, we also are amazed and, when we think of the implications of resurrection, are filled with terror about the future. We long for the discerning word, and for the confirming spirit.

Therefore let us pray, as we move into our baptismal service, for the wind and word beyond the waters. Let this new life that we commemorate be filled with wisdom and centered by the Spirit's enthusiasm. Rattle our bones together, Lord, so that out of unclean mortal sin we might have the shape of new life. Clothe our bones with flesh and sinews for work and joy. Breathe on us the word that directs our hearts to you and inspire us with the breath of risen life. Lead us, Lord, to a clean life in an unclean world. Help us to wholeness when crosses fragment our souls. Bind us with the saints and let us lean on one another as we lean on you. Take away our hearts of stone and give us hearts of Christian flesh formed by thy word and in which thy spirit burns forever without being consumed. O Lord who makes death an empty tomb and who fills us with amazement and fear, we are on the way to you in Galilee. Amen.

This sermon was for Easter Vigil of 1994, preached in Robinson Chapel on April 2, 1994.

14. BUILDINGS AND THE WAY

Read and reflect on 2 Corinthians 4:13–5:5, John 14:1-11.

The principal topic of both of the texts for today is the resurrection, and neither text says plainly what that is. Because the topic is very difficult and I am only a visitor, I shall leave it to Dean Browne to explain at his leisure. I want instead to focus on a subsidiary topic in both texts, namely divine architecture. Jesus used the image of being in God's house with many dwelling places to explain being in the presence of the Father. Paul too said that joining with Jesus in the presence of God means entering the house that God has provided and that we already possess, eternal and in heaven. Now, understanding the resurrection is already complicated in just these two texts by a bewildering array of images—travels to heaven, old and new bodies, Jesus' oneness with God, short-lived troubles versus long-range glory, physical death versus spiritual death, and mortal life versus eternal life. Why do both Paul and John complicate things even more with the architectural image? And isn't it a mischievous image? Hasn't it been used as a simile for our bodies, to suggest the unhealthy conclusion that we relate to our bodies as a temporary tenant to a house?

Things can be put in perspective when we recall that the divine architect is one of the three principal images of God as creator in the Hebrew Bible. Perhaps its most extensive development is in God's speech to Job from the whirlwind in which God asks where Job was when God laid the foundations and measured out the floor plan and elevations of the universe (Job 38). The other two major images are God as potter, as in the second chapter of Genesis, where God makes a clay doll and breathes life into it, and God as king unfolding nature by proclamation, from chaos to light to time to space to land to plants to beasts to us, as in the first chapter of Genesis or even more succinctly in the 96th Psalm. You will recall from the psalm that when the divine king unfolds nature—the depths and the heights, seas and dry land—we turn out to be the sheep of his pasture. When God is potter, we are clay statues whistling with God's breath. I cannot speak for you, but I am not flattered by either sheep or statues as images of the human. On the other hand, God the architect makes the cosmos a house for people in which people can be kings and potters and many other things. That's the power of the architecture image.

With regard to resurrection imagery, the metaphor of changing from an earthly to a heavenly body shares the limitation of sheep and dolls: it does not address us as human. By contrast, the residents of God's house are people; and Jesus and Paul insist upon the point.

Our texts today speak of the heavenly house which, by our inhabiting, puts us in the presence of the Father, the Creator-Architect. Paul contrasted this with our measly earthly houses, which the New Revised Standard Version translates as mere "tents." Resurrection for Paul is going from a tent to a divine mansion. But he juxtaposed this with the change from our old earthly body in which we groan and suffer temporarily to a new and eternal body of glory. Furthermore Paul likened the action of changing bodies or moving from tent to mansion to either taking off the old body and putting on the new one or to putting the new one on over the old one; that is a metaphor concerning clothing and being vested. Houses, bodies, clothes—I suppose Paul wanted the Corinthians not to believe resurrection is any one of these things, but something like them all.

Jesus' argument in John's Gospel is even more complicated. He began by representing God's heavenly house as elsewhere, to which he will go shortly and from which he will return later to find the disciples and take them there. This accords with the common theme that resurrection is something that will happen later, after death; Paul expressed the same theme. But by the end of the passage Jesus had abandoned the house metaphor and asserted that the Father was in him now, and had been all the time Jesus had been with the disciples. By being with Jesus, the disciples were already in the presence of the Father. There is no need for a heavenly journey to some other place later, with a subsequent return. A journey is involved, of course, but it is Jesus' journey on which he had brought his disciple, his Tao, his Way, his love, his mind, his works and deeds. Jesus complained that the disciples did not know that by being with

Jesus on his journey they were already in the presence of the Father, just as if they had gone to God's house.

Paul made a similar point in Colossians 3. Christians at Colossae have already died with Christ, have already been raised with Christ, are now in the presence of the Father, and therefore should pull their lives together and start behaving like Christian disciples. Whatever future reference it has, for Paul resurrection also has a present reference because of who Jesus was in the past and of our present relationship to Jesus.

Now we can see the architectural images of our two texts in a new and compelling light. If dwelling in God's house, in the presence of the Father, is not only later but now, not up somewhere but in Corinth and Colossae and Cambridge, the heavenly house is the cosmos of the divine architect. We are in it; but like even the disciples, we are likely to be unaware of God's presence. How do we dwell in God's house so as to be aware of the Father? By undertaking the Way of Jesus. We dwell with God through Jesus' journey, which is to carry on his identity and extend his ministry into our neighborhood.

Jesus said (John 14:6), "I Am the Way," the path where those who walk it are in the full presence of the Father. Jesus said, "I Am the Truth," where God is fully known and our own deeds brought to light. Jesus said, "I Am the Life," that lifts into God's life all earthly bodies, tents, and tattered clothes, diseases, disasters, old age, and crucifixions. Jesus' I Am is God's being shown to Moses, the Infinite fit into a finite Way begun by Jesus with his disciples and now open to us.

As your preacher, I proclaim to you Jesus' Way and invite you, no matter where you are, to enter onto it more fully. Come to Jesus' Way without reservation and, like the disciples, learn to see God. Become a more thorough disciple in your practice of his Way. Take on his heart habit by habit and you will learn to love more. Take on the mind of Christ bit by bit and you will better learn God's truth. Take on the work of Christ, deed by deed, and you will better learn God's power.

When we join with Jesus' friends in worship, the Father is among us. When we join with Christians in Christ's Body, we are resurrected into Christ's Way. From the standpoint fixed on present troubles and looming death, resurrection includes hope for future glory. But the Way that is Truth and Life is now, not only later; the disciples had been on it before they understood. The Way has been trod from Corinth to Cambridge. The Way is here where Christians pray and serve. This is the House of God through which comes the Way. The Way of Jesus and his friends is resurrected life. Resurrection can be seen here, touched in our gathering, tasted in our Eucharist. Here is the feast of the Way. Let Christ not say to us, "Have I been with you all this time, Philip, and you still do not know me?" We are in the presence of the Father: come let us feast in resurrection faith. Thanks be to God. Amen.

In the spring of 1994 I had a brief sabbatical the Easter term at Cambridge University in England. The Dean of the Chapel at Trinity College there, Arnold Browne, graciously invited me to assist him in services and share the preaching. This sermon was preached on May 1, 1994, which was my birthday. The service was attended by my good friends from the United States, Lois and Donald Treese; they afterward sent a photograph of me standing in Anglican attire in front of the centuries-old stone of the Chapel building.

15. How My Mind Has Changed

Read and reflect on Deuteronomy 28:1-14, Mark 4:1-20.

The topic for this sermon series seemed easy when I accepted Dean Browne's kind invitation. Then last week Reverend Sheldrake preached on the philosophy of changing one's mind, which is what I had thought to do because my training is in philosophy. So next I considered speaking autobiographically about my own changes of mind, which is probably what Dean Browne had in mind in the first place. That should have been easy because I change my mind so much. But sermons are supposed to be edifying and expressive of the gospel, and there is nothing edifying about a fickle head. So I turned to the lectionary selections for the day, which is where sermons should begin anyway, and found there both a type for my own story and the gospel.

The Deuteronomy passage is about faithfulness to God and to the covenant. It offers a prescription for what we can do in order to flourish—that is, live in obedience to God's commands and worship God alone, no other gods. The good news here is that in the chaos of life there is something we can do in order to flourish, something God gives us to do. Deuteronomy expresses the qualities of human flourishing with unequalled poignancy:

> Blessed shall you be in the city, and blessed shall you be in the field. Blessed shall be the fruit of your womb, the fruit of your ground, and the fruit of your livestock, both the increase of your cattle and the issue of your flock. . . .The LORD will make you the head, and not the tail; you shall be only at the top, and not at the bottom—if you obey the commandments of the LORD your God. (Deuteronomy 28:3-13)

To flourish is to be fruitful, to have work rewarded, to have affairs come to fruition, reach maturity, and add together, yielding blessings in the city and in the field, each thing enjoying its season. If we live attuned to God, in whatever version of the covenant structures that attunement for us, we shall be only at the top and not at the bottom. Deuteronomy's great idea is that God will reward those attuned to him with life's fulfillments. Under the blessing wing of a benevolent God our flourishing is in our own hands despite the appearance of life's chaos. As a youth I believed this, as most of us do. If only we are faithful and cultivate a purity of love and obedience, God will bless our lives and cause us to flourish in due season.

Then when I was twenty-seven, my daughter died, at the age of four months, six days after open-heart surgery. Before the operation my wife and I prayed with purity and passion. In the six days after the operation we committed ourselves daily to anything and everything that might save her or care for her with physical or mental impairments. Her heartbeat stopped thirty-three times and after the thirty-fourth time could not be restored.

One expects the death of parents in due season and can accept the death of an adult, even if untimely, because struggling with disease and enemies and the accidents of labor and society are part of what adult life is about. But the death of a small child in the days of modern medicine, before she has a chance for a career or a developed identity, is the very contradiction of blessing or flourishing. I know no grief more stunning, more wrong, than the death of a small child. More of you here tonight than one might imagine understand what I mean.

Now my wife and I were sinners, of course, but not great ones. Fickle people cannot get organized to commit great evil, and junior academics huff and puff about big ideas but really have little consequence. We were more faithful than bad and deserved better. Deuteronomy had a great idea about God making the pious come out on top, but it is false. Simply false. That was the first change of mind to which I wish to witness.

Had I paid proper attention to Jesus' parable of the sower, that wrenching of religious sensibility might not have been so hard. Jesus does not say that everyone has a chance to take the word to heart and flourish in salvation. Some of us are fertile soil, but others of us are placed to be dominated by our desires and passions, yet others have too few resources to handle the pains and burdens of life, and others will be drawn into evil currents despite God's call.

We must be very careful about the perspective with which we address this parable. As applied subjectively to ourselves or others, we do not know what kind of soil we are. We cannot assume from the struggles of faith that we are simply destined like seed on the footpath to be drawn into evil, or that like stony soil our resources are too weak to withstand stress, or that like thorny ground we cannot sort our desires and passions and order them to love. We cannot use the parable as an excuse for abandoning the path of faith when it becomes difficult, for we may turn out in the end to be fertile soil after all. By the same token, we cannot congratulate ourselves if religion feels good to us because we might be barren after all. The word calls to our heart, the seed is planted, and God gives the growth.

But from an objective perspective Jesus' parable does explain why several kinds of people do not flourish in the religious life even though the seeds are planted by parents, pastors, and friends. In Jesus' account, the reasons for failure are like natural conditions: hard-packed soil, thin soil, chocked soil; likewise crops fail for lack of water, fires ravage fields, volcanoes erupt on cities, migrating peoples seek a home and take someone else's. The fragile niche for human life in earth's ecology will not last when the expanding gases of creation take new forms; and children die from the machinery of disease, not from their parents' limitations in holiness. Deuteronomy had a great idea, but it is false. Jesus was uncompromising in his natural realism. Remember the things *he* blessed in *his* beatitudes.

What then is Jesus' gospel? It has a different topic than seems uppermost in Deuteronomy. For Deuteronomy, the topic is what God has done and what we can do in order for us to flourish. For Jesus the topic is not us except secondarily, but God's love and loveliness. Jesus did not say, Be faithful and your kingdom will flourish. He said, This is God's kingdom, so wake up and be faithful. Can we imagine this? Can our twentieth–century imaginations, shaped by the evils of mass wars, by the hypocrisy of so much religion, by the impersonality of the scientific picture, by the knowledge that our world is but an intricate clump of gases and human history but a brief cosmic chain reaction, make plausible Jesus' claim that it still is first God's kingdom? Can we imagine that the earth is the Lord's without displacing suffering and evil and without claiming that human history is meaningful beyond its internal workings? Can we imagine God's love and loveliness without insisting that the righteous flourish in Deuteronomy's way? Can we imagine that God, whom Jesus said to love with all our heart and mind and soul and strength, this lover of our souls, has created a universe that does not run with a moral story but in which morality is limited to human obligations? These are the questions for the Christian mind of our time, not for my mind only.

A few weeks after our daughter died I was reading page proofs for my first book; that kind of mechanical work was a solace. The book was about divine creation, and I was jolted to a stop at a passage expressing the sort of point just made, that God's world is often painful and does not run on rewards and punishments. The point of course is old and orthodox and I knew it without understanding it. The passage in my text concluded with the quotation, "The LORD gave and the LORD has taken away; blessed be the name of the LORD" (Job 1:21). Could I still say that? It took several days of spiritual agony to decide whether to leave that line in or take it out. In the end I left it in, and began a new change of mind that continues more than twenty-five years later.

Let me witness to you about that change of mind as a problem for modern imagination. This part of the Christian faith requires reaching back into the Bible for images that can realistically shape our understanding of God's relation to this vast cosmos, our small place, and our own short stories. There are many images besides Jesus' parable of the sower for overturning Deuteronomy's prescription for coming out on top, for instance those in Job and in Jesus' beatitudes. But what are the positive images? One clue lies in Jesus' Great Commandment, half of which, about loving God, I have already cited; the other half of course is to love our neighbors.

The problem for the late-twentieth-century imagination in loving God is that we begin, if we begin, in fear and awe. More than any other age we understand the vastness of the cosmos, the almost infinite complexity of small things that live, and the sublime impersonality of it all. The sublimity of the cosmos shimmers forth God's glory like shaken foil, as Hopkins said, but it is fearsome, awesome, holy, not even partly tameable by the straightforward attribution of human moral intentions. Modern atheism among sensitive persons is not so much a failure to perceive God but a denial of what is perceived, a plea that the terrifying cosmos so negligent of human scale be not the work of a God who might save. Yet Jesus' parables disabuse us of the dream that God is nice. How can our imaginations move from fear to love of that fierce God?

Jesus said he himself is the Way to the love of God. I have found that over the years devotion to the image of Jesus in his person, teachings, and the representations of the Christian tradition have led me to be able to imagine God's fierce loveliness. It was difficult at first because of confusions with questions about the historical Jesus, the hermeneutics of the texts, and other very important problems with which I am professionally engaged. Over time I have come to see that devotional commitment to

Jesus in images is not the same as knowledge about Jesus but rather is the means to making the imagination more holy. Holiness in imagination is accepting numinous terror and transforming fear to love, as Augustine said. For me now, Jesus is the lord of the dance, the dance of expanding gases, the dance of the seasons, the dance of life and death, creation and destruction, struggle, teaching, healing, crucifixion, who calls us into the dance and dances us home. The fierce creator into whom Jesus leads us is infinite in loveliness. To be there in imagination, however briefly, is bliss. Perhaps others get there by dancing after Siva or Maitreya or Chuang Tzu or with Rumi's dervishes—Christians have no monopoly on stretching imagination to bliss. But I belong to the cult of Jesus and get there lamely dancing Jesus' way of crucifixion and resurrection.

Shaping your life around the images of Jesus' way also helps resolve the practical questions of how to live in a vast, impersonal cosmos, namely through being a good neighbor. We learn to love our neighbors, not humanity, and to improve the institutions within reach. There is no guarantee that grand plans will be successful or that even small good works will be rewarded. Crucifixion, remember, is half the dominant image for understanding how life goes. The other half is resurrection, which is not coming out on top in Deuteronomy's sense but coming out in God. The human scale of moral obligations and striving for a good and fruitful existence gives finite meaning to our lives, and there is little more to finite meaning than our limited achievements and failures in this regard. But our finite lives are given infinite meaning when raised into the infinite life of God. The topic, then, as Jesus would urge, is not us but God. Our finite fulfillment is to follow Jesus and do the best we can, win or lose, until we die. Our infinite fulfillment is to dance with Jesus through fire and water, across the abyss and into the light, into the Holy One of Israel, fierce and lovely beyond measure.

Sermons should end with an invitation, and so I invite you to enter or to continue on the Way of Jesus. It embraces loved sinners with loved saints, holy grief with holy joy, a cosmos sublime in its impersonal stretch with a moral life that is its own only reward. Conforming ourselves to the mind of Christ, we can dance home to God. That is how my mind has changed. Amen.

Trinity College, Cambridge, has an Evensong sermon series each term exploring a given topic. During my Easter term visiting semester the topic was "How my mind has changed," and I delivered this sermon on May 8, 1994.

16. ASCENSION

Read and reflect on Acts 1:1-11, Matthew 28:16-20.

Two strikingly different traditions of the church are represented by texts for this Feast of the Ascension. Matthew, for instance, locates the postresurrection events in Galilee, with the Great Commission, which was just read, being delivered on a Galilean mountain. Luke, on the other hand, in his Gospel and in the book of Acts, locates the postresurrection events in and around Jerusalem, according to him, the final commission and ascension took place near Bethany on Mount Olivet, which was then a Jerusalem suburb. Both traditions have an irreducible and essential point to make and each should be meditated upon without fixation.

From our standpoint as Christians seeking understanding and guidance, the greatest difference is that in Matthew's account Jesus promises to be with the disciples "always, to the end of the age"; whereas in Luke's Gospel and again in Acts, Jesus is shown leaving. Obviously the historical Jesus left, and the tradition has reconciled Matthew's text to this by understanding Jesus' continuing presence to be in a spiritual sense. An important difference remains, however. Matthew has given rise to a tradition of piety emphasizing a continuing personal relation of individuals and the church with Jesus, whereas Luke began the tradition of piety emphasizing the Holy Spirit as the mode in which God is present among us.

Luke's point was not merely that Jesus is absent and God is present in the Holy Spirit (after Pentecost). It was also that by his ascension Jesus established the disciples, their work, and the world in a positive relation with heaven. Their fulfillment shall be in heaven, and their present life should be regarded in that larger context. The ascension, though a separation, establishes a connection. Now what can this mean to us late-twentieth-century Christians with such a different spiritual geography, searching the scriptures to understand God in our own situation? Jesus rejected the disciples' overfamiliar desire to understand providence and its timing, saying "The times and occasions are set by my Father's own authority, and it is not for you to know when they will be." Rather, the disciples should consider their task to be witnessing to Jesus throughout the world, come what may, he said. This puts us in a proper humble place and marks the distance between God and us symbolically traversed in the ascension. On the other hand, Jesus promised that we in our humble work will also be transformed by the Holy Spirit. God will cross the distance to come to us so that our humble work will be God's work, shaped and cheered by heaven itself. The worship of the church after Pentecost does indeed have access to the ascended Christ; and we enact that access, that commerce with heaven, in liturgies such as this. By ascending, Jesus takes us to the Father whose providence is inscrutable but who welcomes us into the vastness of the divine life. By sending the Spirit, Jesus gives our ordinary lives not only purpose but divine joy. So by meditating on the symbols of Jesus' mediating journey we not only have our minds shaped to God's Trinitarian nature, always a good thing for God's faithful. We also uncover the complexities of our place: humble but set in heaven, bound to our time but fulfilled in God's time, witnesses to Jesus but friends of God, enduring crucifixion but living in resurrection, anxious in work but patient in joy, absent from Jesus but filled with his Spirit. This complex place is our home. It is in God, and Jesus' ascension takes us there. Matthew was not wrong that Jesus will be with us to the end of the age. Amen.

For a Methodist from the American Midwest such as myself, however enthusiastic about the revival of profound liturgy in The United Methodist Church, the Anglican celebration of the liturgical year is a wondrous novelty. I have long been a lectionary preacher, which means the texts are tied to the liturgical seasons. But at Trinity, we celebrated not only Easter Feast but the Ascension and Pentecost, with all the intervening preparation and retrospection. The effect on me was to focus intensely on the heart of Christian doctrine, which is made or broken by how it can handle the symbols connecting Easter to Pentecost, when Jesus passes the responsibility from himself to the church. I was privileged to preach this sermon on the Feast of the Ascension at Trinity College on May 12, 1994.

17. WHERE IS THE BODY OF CHRIST?

Read and reflect on Ephesians 4:1-13, Luke 24:45-53.

In the parceling out of the ministry of the preached Word this term, the Dean gets Pentecost next Sunday and I get the ascension today. In one sense he has the more dangerous topic because Pentecost, the coming of the Spirit, is a real phenomenon. It's something you can see and feel, by which you can get burned, become transported. I hope that you have encountered that phenomenon yourselves. If you have, you can check up on what the Dean says, which is always dangerous for a preacher.

In another sense the ascension is a more dangerous topic because it is an anti-phenomenon, an absence. What can one say about an absence? You can see why preachers like the Easter resurrection topics: the buried Jesus becomes the phenomenon of the risen Christ, engaging people in palpable ways. Yet according to Christian doctrine and symbolism, the post-Easter appearances were but a forty-day layover on a journey whose real destination was heaven. After the forty days, the risen Christ has left. Given what we know of our world, Jesus is not here in an empirical sense, not to be found in any bazaar or mountain cave. In a deeper, thoroughly orthodox, symbolic sense, ours is a world characterized by the absence of God as a palpable interactive agent. So if Christianity were to say that Jesus is still around as a very old guru, we would know Christianity to be an illusion. What does Jesus' ascension, his moving on, his taking leave, his absence, teach us about God and ourselves?

To begin with Luke's account, we note that Jesus gives his disciples a commission. The ministry Jesus had begun personally is now transferred to his disciples and down the line to us. The ascension means the transference of responsibility for God's special work from Jesus to the church. It was not a mere loss of the personal presence of Jesus. It meant a new reality for the disciples, their coming of age, if you will.

Consider for a moment the content of Jesus' Great Commission. He began by opening the disciples' eyes to the scriptures so that henceforth they should understand themselves, their world, and their mission in the biblical outlook. Specifically, the disciples were to understand themselves as followers of the Christ, the Messiah, who suffered and then rose from the dead—going on, to be sure, to ascend into heaven. That is, the disciples were personally and corporately to be identified in terms of their relation to Jesus as the Christ. Their mission, said Jesus, was to preach repentance and the forgiveness of sins in his name. That the preaching should be in the name of Jesus joins it to Jesus' own preaching about the kingdom of God, namely that God loves us, forgives our sins, and restores us when repentance takes the form of faith. Jesus' own resurrection, understood scripturally, confirms that this is indeed the kingdom of God, appearances to the contrary notwithstanding. When Luke retells the story of the ascension in the first chapter of Acts, Jesus says that the disciples should be witnesses to him, his teachings, his work, his resurrection, and, obviously, his ascension.

One more point to notice about the Great Commission is its extent: the witness begins in Jerusalem but is to go out to all nations. Whereas Jesus himself had been uncomfortable talking even to Canaanites, focusing his own efforts on the lost children of Israel, the disciples are supposed to proclaim God's kingdom of repentance, forgiveness, new life, and love across the whole world. Jesus is not the only one who leaves in the ascension: the disciples too are sent away from home, to be absent from their familiars and wanderers in a strange land. So the first point I wish to make about the ascension is that Jesus' leaving is the condition for the transformation of the disciples into apostles, his witnesses, with a responsibility for the ministry of the good news of new life begun by Jesus in Galilee but to be taken by them and their successors all over the world.

My second point is to conjure with Paul's wild image of the cosmic Christ. Paul did not say merely that Jesus left the disciples and ascended into heaven on a cloud. In a rush of metaphysical excitement Paul sang, "He ascended into the heights with captives in his train; he gave gifts to men." And he continued in the lecture mode, "Now, the word 'ascended' implies that he also descended to the lowest level, down to the very earth. He who descended is no other than he who ascended far above all heavens, so that he might fill the universe" (Ephesians 4:8-10 NEB). If Luke treated the resurrection as a mere way station on the journey to heaven, Paul's Jesus overshoots heaven to go even higher. And Paul assumed a transcendent pre-Incarnation heavenly identity to Jesus so that he had to descend to earth in birth before it would be possible to ascend. If that puzzles you, be sure to come back next Advent when Dean Browne will preach on the Incarnation.

The point I wish to draw out now is that Paul takes the ascension to be the divine reconnection of the cosmos, heaven with earth. Back and forth Jesus goes like the shuttle on a loom, weaving a continuous fabric joining us with God. The Apostles' Creed extends the geography, saying that Jesus also descended below the earth into hell, reconnecting the dead and even the damned. Paul's cosmic Christ does a cosmic dance, "so that he might fill the universe." What does this mean? It means that if salvation seems far off, there still is a way to get there. It means that if the ancient Jewish messianic identity of Jesus seems antique, quaint, and not part of the late-twentieth-century world, still the best way to understand ourselves today is through an extension of that identity. It means that if our own lives are finite, fragmented, a bunch of incomplete stories, there still is a way to weave them into the infinite, whole, and glorious life of God. It means that the kingdom of our world, filled with "wars and alarms," is still on the way within the kingdom of God. What is that way? It is the way of those commissioned disciples, witnessing to Jesus' power of repentance, forgiveness, faith, and love. When Christ fills the universe, there is no place from which he is absent, no way away from God. As Paul put it in another place, "For I am convinced that neither death, nor life, nor angels, nor rulers, nor things present, nor things to come, nor powers, nor height, nor depth, nor anything else in all creation, will be able to separate us from the love of God in Christ Jesus our Lord" (Romans 8:38-39).

My final point is to call attention to Paul's remark that Jesus, in ascending and descending, brought gifts. "And these were his gifts: some to be apostles, some prophets, some evangelists, some pastors and teachers, to equip God's people for work in his service, to the building up of the body of Christ" (Ephesians 4:11-12 NEB). This, of course, is Paul's perspective on the Great Commission, except that he presents it as Jesus' actually making his disciples into effective extensions of his ministry. Paul was writing before the division of separate ministries into lay and ordained; in other places he lists even more ministerial offices. And the context of his writing to the Ephesians was some controversy over competitions among different ministerial offices. He was pleading with the Ephesians to "live up to your calling," to be humble, gentle, patient, forbearing, charitable, making "fast with bonds of peace the unity which the Spirit gives" (4:1-3 NEB), all of which was evidently problematic in the Ephesians church. To emphasize the importance of unity he lifted up "one hope," "one Lord, one faith, one baptism, one God and Father of all, who is over all and through all and in all" (4:5-6 NEB). Jesus' ministry has so many parts, with the need for so many different kinds of people, so many kinds of witness, that the problem is to keep them, us, together.

But look at the image that emerged from his legitimating of differences and call to unity: we are the body of Christ. As the body has many members, so there are many ministries. Diversely "to equip God's people for work in his service," Paul said, is "the building up of the body of Christ" (4:12 NEB). What an amazing transformation of symbols! Paul's discussion of ascension comes right in the middle of his plea for unity of different ministries in the body of Christ. For Paul the ascension is not so much about Jesus being hauled body and soul up to heaven but about transforming us inconstant and competitive would-be disciples into Christ's true body, spreading to all nations and lasting through all history. The point is the same as Luke's: the ascension means that the disciples are transformed so as to be the responsible bearers of Jesus' identity and ministry. Jesus' ascension means that we come of age. Paul said, "So shall we all at last attain to the unity inherent in our faith and our knowledge of the Son of God—to mature manhood, measured by nothing less than the full stature of Christ" (4:13 NEB). But Paul gives Luke's point apocalyptic intensity: when Jesus ascends to fill the universe, his disciples, from the first ones down to us, become his resurrected body. That is the scriptural way to understand our situation: we are the body of Christ, diversely bearing witness to God's kingdom of love and forgiveness.

I hope you have sympathy for my homiletical pain in forbearing to encroach upon the Dean's Pentecost sermon next week; the pain is the mild converse of what the original disciples must have felt in the time from their last sight of Jesus until the Spirit came to them in that upper room. They were like adolescents with a big new body and no mind how to use it. We, however, know the full measure of maturity and seek it in the way of Christ. Our Jesus having risen and ascended, we each take up some portion of his life if we are disciples. I invite any here who are not to become disciples and participate in the full measure of maturity. Properly to grasp and celebrate his ascension, we have but to take Christ's Creed upon ourselves, as we are about to do. Amen.

The most difficult aspect of an Anglican sermon for a Methodist is its brevity. Ten minutes tops, and you should know that the last two minutes do not command attention. Nevertheless, Anglicans have many more services a week than most Methodists, and even though Dean Browne and I alternated preachments, themes could be carried over from one service to another within a short space of time. The drawback to this is that the same people are not in attendance from one service to the next, save for the faithful choir. This gave new meaning to the phrase "preaching to the choir." This sermon was preached at Trinity College on May 15, 1994, Ascension Sunday. Immediately following the sermon the service continued with the Apostles' Creed.

18. WHITE ROBES, RED BLOOD, WIPED TEARS

Read and reflect on Revelation 7:9-17, Psalm 23, Acts 9:36-43, John 10:22-30.

When I was a child, there were many things about the Christian religion that seemed mixed up to me. On one stained-glass window in my church at home there was a huge picture of Jesus the Good Shepherd, cradling a lamb in his arm. Across the church was another window showing a huge lamb with a flag crooked in his leg that people assured me was also Jesus. Well, which was he? A shepherd or a lamb? I rooted for the shepherd role, myself. Then there was the matter of locomotion. Jesus obviously liked to walk, which he did up and down mountains and from town to town; he even walked on water. Why then did he ride a donkey into Jerusalem on Palm Sunday? More puzzling, why did he try to ride a donkey mother and her colt at once? Was he showing off? Wasn't that unnecessarily cruel to the little colt? And speaking of walking on water, if God could arrange that, why did he go to the trouble of drying out the Red Sea with an all-night wind when he could simply have walked the Israelites across and left the Egyptians to hunt for boats? When I was a child, I thought someone ought to get the story straight. As Reverend Oh will tell you, God has blessed me with a paycheck for working on these problems ever since, now fifty years later.

To my childish mind, the silliest claim in the Bible was that you could wash your clothes in blood and have them come out white. My mother had negative views about getting blood on clothes, and at the time I thought her concern was with the fact that blood stains do not wash out; they leave red marks on the clothes forever. In reality she probably was more concerned with where the blood came from—my knees or fingers—than with where it went. But she became very upset when I proposed one day to wash my shirt in chicken blood from a garbage can to see if it would come out white. My problem as a child was a limited symbolic imagination. I tried to make literal sense of everything. My problem as an adult is to understand the symbols in their spiritual meaning, which I want us to reflect on.

Recall the scene as set in the passage from Revelation 7. Jesus is symbolized as the Lamb, standing before the throne of God. "And there was a great multitude that no one could count, from every nation, from all tribes and peoples and languages, standing before the throne and before the Lamb, robed in white, with palm branches in their hands." The multitude is worshiping God with songs of praise and gestures of bowing while the witness is told who they are: they are the ones "who have come out of the great ordeal; they have washed their robes and made them white in the blood of the Lamb."

Now this passage is a symbolic interpretation of the life of the Christian church after the resurrection of Jesus. We can easily identify with the fact that there is a great multitude, beyond counting, from every nation, from all tribes and people, and from all languages. Some of you will recognize this as a symbolic version of the Pentecost story in Acts, when the Holy Spirit came upon a crowd of Christian disciples who began to witness in a great variety of languages to an even larger crowd of people from all over the world. Christianity is not a religion only for people speaking Jesus' language but, from the earliest times, has brought people together from different nations and cultures. Much of the surrounding material in the book of Revelation talks about the twelve tribes of Israel. But our passage here is explicit about mentioning those tribes and also other peoples from other nations and cultures, languages other than Hebrew.

This congregation, a Korean American church, is particularly fortunate because the multiplicity of languages and cultures is built in. You might think of that sometimes as a problem. There is comfort in sameness. But the all-Korean churches in Seoul and the all-white or all-black churches in the United States miss the point of diversity among the saved. They are apt to forget just who it is who praises God: it is a multitude of many peoples and languages. Congregations of a single culture are likely to forget how important it is to be a good neighbor, because being a neighbor to people like yourself seems culturally easy. You remember, however, that Jesus' example of the neighbor was the good Samaritan who befriended his cultural enemy, the Jew.

120

What happened on Pentecost? The Holy Spirit came to the disciples, all of whom were Palestinian Jews, who then began to translate the gospel into as many languages as were spoken by the large crowd from across the globe. Christianity is a religion that never fits completely into any culture but exists rather in the ministry of translation from one culture to another. The multitude bowing before the throne of God and the Lamb were singing: "Amen! Blessing and glory and wisdom and thanksgiving and honor and power and might be to our God forever and ever! Amen." There are words for that in every language, in Korean and English as well as in the Greek in which the book of Revelation was written. You who are moving between cultures, who are translating from Korean to English to Korean again, are privileged to be especially attuned to what true worship is like: singing songs of praise together in many ways. The praising of God in song and dance are one of the two things the great multitude had in common, standing before the throne.

The other thing the people had in common was their white robes, the ones that had been washed in the blood of the Lamb and still came out white, to my great puzzlement. This symbolism is puzzling enough that even the author of Revelation believed he had to put in an explanation, namely that all the people with the white robes had come through the Great Ordeal. Do I have to say what the ordeal of life is? Of course not. We have all seen it. But let me mention what the book of Revelation says. Our text for today occurs in the middle of the famous discussion of the Seven Seals, between the sixth and seventh seal. The seals mark the character of the ordeal of life.

The first seal, with the white horse and rider, is for war and the passion for conquering. This century has been one of the bloodiest in the history of war. Every continent on earth has been the scene of wars fought by soldiers from every other continent. In this century we have learned to go to war with tanks, airplanes, submarines, rockets, missiles, gas, napalm, and nuclear bombs. The lust to conquer has devastated cities and all who live in them, and jungles with all their teeming life. Korea has been fought over in whole or in part by Japanese, Americans, Chinese, and by divided families of Koreans themselves. War is the first ordeal, and it leaves people stained in blood, combatants and innocent alike.

The second seal, with the red horse and rider, takes away peace and brings violence. As if direct war were not enough, we slaughter one another with cars on the highways. We poison one another with pollution. We abuse our children and batter those whom we love. Our streets are not safe. Our homes are subject to robbery and vandalism. Our public places are defaced. Species of animals are extinguished, forests ruined, streams turned to sludge. After the bombing of children in Oklahoma City, we know that the red horse and rider have come our way. Fury, violence, and destruction are the second ordeal; and they leave us all stained with blood.

The third seal unleashes the black horse and rider who bring famine and poverty. Rich as the Earth is, millions of people are hungry. In Africa and other parts of the world people are starving because of war's destruction of their economies. In America millions of children live in poverty. In many parts of the world the economic conditions are so bad that even hard work and intelligent use of resources cannot bring improvement. Some people lose the chance they have. Other people never have a chance. How thankful we few are who through work, sacrifice, and risk are able to move ahead; but how few we are. The third seal is broken, and in its ordeal, children's hunger is a bloody stain on us all.

The fourth seal's horse and rider are pale and green, and they are death. Although some of us can escape hunger, none can escape death. We bury our grandparents and our parents, our aunts and uncles. Sometimes we bury our brothers and sisters and cousins. Some of us even have the horror to bury our children. Even with good genes, high-tech medicine, and loads of ginseng, every one of us will die someday. None escapes the pale rider. The ordeal of death drains red blood to bleach bones white.

The fifth seal has no horse and rider but opens the graves of the martyrs for God. Martyrdom is the lot of a far smaller band than those whose ordeals come from the Four Horsemen of the Apocalypse. Yet have we not known martyrs, witnesses for God, who suffered in our own time? I remember the day Gandhi was shot, and Martin Luther King, Jr. My wife's family had a martyr in Korea: Ethel Underwood, whose husband was president of Yonsei University, was gunned down in the doorway of her house on the Yonsei campus, for her Christian beliefs. But many Christian families in Korea had relatives who died for their faith. Perhaps some of you remember martyrs and their ordeal, their bloody witness.

The sixth seal opens the monstrosities of nature, earthquakes and eclipses of the sun, bloody moons and falling stars, the explosion of mountains and the shifting of islands. The rich and powerful, like the poor and weak, seek safety from destruction; but the earth trembles like the wrath of God, and we know that our puny and selfish hopes and fears do not count for much of anything when subjected to forces on a cosmic scale.

The judgment of God does not attend to excuses and is not moved by human efforts of sacrifice and propitiation. What is demanded of us is justice; and when the end comes, we are who we are and nothing more. The sixth ordeal, in which the sky rolls up like a scroll, subjects us to the blood of God's vast creation and its inhuman powers.

With the opening of the six seals the author of Revelation rehearses the elements of the Great Ordeal that defines the human condition. To go through any one part or all is to come through bloodied. I use the term *bloodied* deliberately. It does not mean merely that we are guilty of doing something wrong. Of course many of us do sin directly, in unjust war or in violence or in oppressing the poor. But direct, responsible guilt is not the only problem here. Nor does being bloodied mean merely that we have been hurt physically. Life is filled with accidents, disease, and natural violence that hurt us but do not bloody us in the sense I mean.

To be bloodied in the sense that needs cleansing is to be part of a world that is broken and dirty. All the ordeals, of war and violence, of poverty and death, of martyrdom and destruction, are themselves symbols of a world that is broken and dirty. Underneath it is lovely and beautiful, the fruit of God's creation. But it is distorted and stained, and everything we do is ambiguous. No matter how much good we do, it seems that the good always has a downside, that it hurts somebody, or comes back to haunt us. That is part of the meaning of the scripture from the Acts of the Apostles. The main part of the story is of how Peter brought the holy woman back to life. But the last line of the story is that Peter was staying at the house of Simon the tanner: a tanner is an unclean person who works with dead bodies and skins. Although he exercised God's power to revive the dead, Peter still was stained by association with dead animals who were only preserved.

Now we can see the significance of Jesus as the Lamb of God. According to John's Gospel, in the reading for today, Jesus is the Good Shepherd who lays down his life for the sheep. The hired hands would not risk much for the sheep when the wolf comes; but the Good Shepherd would risk his life. Jesus did that. But as the Lamb of God, Jesus is neither the shepherd or one of the lost sheep. Rather, Jesus is like the Passover lamb. When the children of Israel were in Egypt, God aimed to force Pharaoh to release them by striking dead all the firstborn, both human children and animals. To preserve the Israelites in Egypt from this destruction, they were to kill a lamb and spread its blood on the doorpost to ward off the angel of death. Jesus was like the Passover lamb whose blood warded off death and destruction.

123

But even more, Jesus was like the lamb sacrificed at the temple to purify a ritually stained person, family, or group. The function of sacrifice in the ancient Hebrew religion was not to buy back God's favor. No. It was rather a ritual instituted by God to set right the moral and ritual sins of the people, to purify them from uncleanness and stain. Jesus was like the ritual sacrifice animal sent from God, whose spilled blood set things right again. But this also was only part of the story. For the sin to be atoned by Jesus was not just some moral or ritual stain but a corruption of the whole world, the very fact of war, violence, poverty, death, martyrdom, and destruction. The whole world is diseased and needs a physician. The whole world is broken and needs a new cornerstone. The whole world is unclean and needs to be baptized through death to life. The whole world is ignorant and needs a gospel. The whole world is corrupt and needs to be purified. All of these images gather around Jesus and coalesce in the symbol of the Lamb of God whose sacrificial blood washes away our sins, purifies our world, heals us, instructs us, and gives us new life. The white robes of the multitude symbolize the fact they have been saved and purified. They did not earn the white robes by enduring their ordeals. The ordeals made them dirty. They were made clean by the cosmic act of God in Christ. God forgives our sins, makes our uncleanliness of new account, and gives us new life to start again, however difficult the rest of our life might be.

As a child I was confused: I thought that the point was to dip dirty clothes into a washtub filled with red blood and have them come out miraculously white. But that missed the point of the symbols. The symbol of the Lamb points to the love of God that forgives, cleans, and heals us. The symbol of the white clothes points in our saved state, from which we need to respond to God with praise and thanksgiving. I tell you, my friends, that you are wearing the Lamb's white clothes whether you know it or not. They might look blue, red, green, black, yellow, or brown to the naked eye; but to God and to the eyes of faith, they are white. You might not feel clean; you might feel sinful and dirty, full of guilt and shame, anxious to hide your inmost thoughts. But God has blown through you like an all-knowing wind, has seen all that, and forgiven you. You have been washed by the blood of the Lamb who stands before God's throne, and you should praise God for that. You might not have felt the mountains move or seen the stars fall from the sky, but the Lamb has moved through here and we are free and clean, ready and able, if only we are willing, to follow him.

Revelation compounded my childish imagination even farther when it says, "for the Lamb at the center of the throne will be their shepherd." The Good Shepherd who sacrificed his life for the sheep has become the sacrificial Lamb who in turn is our shepherd. As the Twenty-third Psalm says, and Revelation quotes, he will guide us to the springs of the water of life. And God will wipe away every tear from their eyes.

What does this mean for us? It does not mean that we will escape ordeals. We all face death and war and violence and nature's powers, and maybe the other ordeals as well. We will have many occasions yet to cry and comfort one another. But we know in fact that the Lamb has died for us and awaits us at the throne of God. In God's eyes, even now we are clothed in white and ready for prayer and praise. Although we live day by day and look ahead for the crown and white robes, God lives in eternity, loves in eternity, is praised in eternity, and is to be loved by us now in eternity. I invite you, my friends, to look around and see all the white clothing disguised in other colors. I invite you to bow to our friend Jesus, our Shepherd, our Lamb of God, who has made us clean and has given us new life. I invite you to make your life a hymn of praise and thanksgiving: Blessing and glory and wisdom and thanksgiving and honor and power and might be to our God forever.

The Boston University School of Theology has had many Korean students, and has many now. My own connections with Korea are through my wife whose cousins, the Underwood family, have been in Korea since the 1880s. I have visited there many times and the "Thanksgiving" sermon above was preached in Seoul. But it is a great treat to preach for our students at their parishes in the United States. This sermon was preached on May 7, 1995, at the Zion Korean Methodist Church in Warwick, Rhode Island, where Jung-sun Oh is the pastor and We-hun Chang his associate. I delivered each paragraph, and then the Reverend Oh delivered a Korean translation. The lectionary texts involved highly charged symbols and the translation must be difficult. Alas, I will never know how the translation turned out!

PART FOUR
THE CHURCH AND THE WORLD

Palm

19. DUTY FIRST

Read and reflect on Lamentations 1:1-6, Psalm 137, 2 Timothy 1:1-14, Luke 17:5-10.
Hymns: "Love Divine, All Loves Excelling," 384; "Come, We That Love the Lord," 732; "Thou Hidden Love of God," 414

Once again I am grateful for Dean Thornburg's birthday, for two reasons. The first is that he is one of my favorite people in all the world and a steady run of birthdays is very good for his health. The second is that I am privileged to preach on this day when he and his twin brother, Richard, are off celebrating. But as in previous years I am suspicious of the Sunday the Thornburgs select for their birthday weekend because of the political incorrectness of the text assigned by the lectionary. The lesson from Luke has two main parts, you will have noticed: the benign assurance that true faith grows like a grain of mustard seed and the politically offensive judgment that when your slaves finish in the fields, they should not sit down to eat with you but put on their aprons and serve you—and only after that, when their duty is done, take their own food and drink. You can bet that there will be a thousand lectionary sermons on mustard seeds and faith this morning for every one on the duty of slaves. But is it not the duty of a dean of a theology school to address the hard texts? I am a slave to Jesus: the field in which I work is theology, and my indoor work is preaching. So prepare yourselves for a sermon on the duty of slaves. I beg forgiveness from those whom I might offend because slavery is too close, and ask only that you listen through my words for the Word of God.

We should begin by addressing frankly what is offensive in this passage. First and most obvious is Jesus' assumption that slavery is an unquestioned institution. One of the chief contributions of Christian cultures has been the abolition of slavery. Perhaps abolition took too long in the lands deeply influenced by Christianity. But the evil institution lingers now only in some parts of Africa and Asia, and the human rights movement, which owes so much to Christian ethics, is pressing hard on the practice in those areas. In Jesus' world, slavery was widespread and accepted. The Torah legislates the just treatment of slaves. Both Jesus and Paul give instructions on how slaves ought to behave, as in the passage today from Luke; and Paul uses the status of slavery to describe Jesus in the famous hymn from Philippians according to which Christ humbled himself, took on the form of a slave, and was obedient unto death, rising to glory before whom every knee should bow. We must be against slavery and its oppressing consequences with all our hearts, and yet be ready to learn from what Scripture says about it.

The second offensive element of the Lukan passage is its clear denial of equality or, in other New Testament terms, Jesus' table fellowship. Jesus admitted people of all estates to his table and got in trouble for that. From this has arisen the fundamental Christian notion that God's love includes everyone and that we had better include them in our fellowship as well. The Christian movement disciplines itself to embrace everyone and anyone, no matter how poor, how different, or how repulsive. Moreover, in Jesus' table fellowship, discipline grows to holiness, and acceptance turns to love. Jesus' remarks in the passage under discussion, however, assert that the business of slaves is to serve their masters and only then should they go off and eat, by themselves.

The third offensive element, perhaps the worst, is that the slaves should not only obey but be happy in their obedience. Jesus put it even more strongly when telling the disciples that they were the slaves in question: "So you also, when you have done all that you were ordered to do, say, 'We are worthless slaves; we have done only what we ought to have done!'" In our own criticism of involuntary slavery, by contrast, we now say that anger and resentment are appropriate responses and that cheerful obedience reinforces bondage.

Each of these offensive elements is truly offensive, and especially so to the Christian conscience. Nevertheless, we need to ask what we can learn from Jesus' remark. In what sense are we properly slaves? I have already quoted Jesus' answer: To be a Christian, a disciple of Jesus Christ, is to be a slave to him, whose duties are those of the Christian life. Slavery is not the sole metaphor for discipleship—having faith like a grain of mustard seed is far more popular, and sitting at Jesus' table is comforting to our hurts and also to our sense of democratic equality. But slavery certainly catches attention about the seriousness of discipleship. Jesus' slavery is voluntary, at least on the surface, but very demanding.

The demands come as Christian duties, which Jesus summarized as two: to love God with all your heart, mind, soul, and strength, and to love your neighbor. It is hard to understand how love for God can be commanded, a duty rather than an affection. But Jesus was quite clear about how to love neighbors: Be like the Good Samaritan. Let me recall that illustration for you. The hero of neighborliness was a member of a sometimes persecuted ethnic minority from whom Jews were supposed to segregate themselves. He came upon a Jew who had been mugged and whose own community did not help him. The Samaritan poured oil on his wounds, bandaged them, took him to an inn for rest and attention, and paid his bill, promising to pay whatever else was necessary for his recovery. He did not try to convert the Jew, or insist that the Jew be a good person, or encourage mutual cultural understanding, or expect the Jew to say thank you. He simply saw the beaten man as a person in need and acted to help him, accepting the differences that likely would have made closer friendship difficult. The Samaritan was simply doing his baseline duty, like the slaves Jesus enjoined Christians to be.

There is a political lesson in Jesus' duty of neighborliness. In the Christian and Jewish traditions a nation is known by how it takes care of its poor, sick, and abandoned, the people who are failed or abused by their families and institutions. The American people, I am proud to say, have exhibited since the 1930s a profound generosity of spirit, creating jobs for the poor paid for by the wealthy through a graduated income tax, guaranteeing support for children and for the elderly who otherwise would have no support, caring for the sick and for those traumatized by natural disasters such as floods, earthquakes, and hurricanes. We have even exercised charity toward our enemies, sometimes transforming our foes into close partners. This generosity of spirit has not been consistent or always helpful by any means, and I do not want to exaggerate it. Jesus' Good Samaritan had an efficient economy about him that a nation cannot have, and America has had its share of greed, fear, and vengefulness. But this general attempt at national generosity has expressed a humanity, founded on a religious, ethical vision almost unprecedented in world history.

Our new politics, alas, seems bent on reversing this tradition of neighborly generosity on a national scale. They are cutting back on help for those who are beaten, they blame the victims for walking down a road with robbers, they insist that those whom they help earn their help by working, they demand cultural conformity and gratitude, and they take more glee in pursuing the robbers than helping their victims.

Please understand that I am not advocating uncritical continuation of the federal welfare system. Its purpose always ought to be to bridge people through tough times and get them off welfare into socially productive ways of life. Where the welfare system reinforces dependence, it ought to be changed, no question. When welfare makes people lose their soul, it does not help; it is as if the Samaritan had poured salt rather than oil on the wounds.

Nevertheless, a generous national spirit does not abandon the people who remain poor, alienated, and self-destructive. In particular, it does not call for people to leave welfare for productive work when there is no productive work to which they could go. Welfare will be effective as a bridge to social health only when there are jobs for people who have not worked before, jobs with stability and security that provide a greater human fulfillment than welfare dependency.

Where is Christian duty in this political time? It clearly lies in support of helpful programs that express a generosity of spirit and in opposition to the growing greed and insistence on cultural conformity. This is baseline duty for disciple/slaves to Jesus Christ: Love your neighbor!

But here is the political question of Christian duty: How can this traditional statement of the gospel commandment be reconciled with the political platform of the so-called Christian Right, whom conservative politicians are now courting so sweetly? I don't mean theological conservatives per se, but political conservatives who use Christian theology for shutting down national generosity and care for the needy. I have many friends who pursue the ethic of neighborly generosity but who are not at all disciples of Jesus Christ because, for them, Christianity is identified as the Christian Right. For them, Christianity is the problem. They assume that Christianity is faithfully represented by the cultural parochialism, moral narrowness, ethnic bigotry, exclusivism, and judgmentalism so often associated with the Christian Right. To answer the perplexity of those non-Christian witnesses to Christian charity, we must ask the Christian Right to explain how its policies are neighborly like the Good Samaritan. How does it meet Jesus' demand for a good disciple, namely, like a slave to do what you ought to do for your neighbors, particularly for those not of your family and culture? Where Jesus said "judge not," it judges. Where Jesus practiced fellowship with sinners, it blames sinners. Where Jesus broadened moral vision while intensifying obligation, the Christian Right narrows moral vision and abandons vast areas of social concern to the forces of greed. Where is the slave's obedience in the Christian Right's approach to the elementary duty of Samaritan neighborliness?

This brings us back to the other half of the duty of Christian disciples, namely, to love God, for which many in the Christian Right profess great passion. I agree with the Right that mainline forms of Christianity have sometimes become so preoccupied with neighborliness that loving God slips to the bottom of the agenda of the slave's duties. We might learn from the Right in this respect.

Whereas loving our neighbors is always relative to who our neighbors are, and sometimes our attempts to help do more harm than good, loving God is an absolute thing, commanding all our heart, mind, soul, and strength. It often takes years of obedience in discipleship before we can energize and focus our hearts, minds, souls, and strength enough to love God with consuming passion. Most of us come to Christianity looking for what God can do for us, and in this posture are thankful for God's love of us. Once in the church and seeking to take on and fulfill the duties of disciple/slaves, we concentrate on what we can do for God: This is ministry and neighborliness. But in the end, loving God is what makes religion religious, and neighborliness is its natural consequence. Loving God is what makes disciple/slaves say, "We are only doing our duty." Loving God is hard to learn, harder than learning to love a friend; but it is the only thing that gives ultimate meaning to life. Loving God is the most fulfilling thing we can do, but it makes our own fulfillment a trivial pursuit. Loving God gives us true individuality, but we do it in the company of a great cloud of witnesses. Loving God lights a vision that calls forth our heart, mind, soul, and strength and surrenders them to God. Loving God, God's glory commands us; we cannot say no; and we are never more free than when we give ourselves in ecstatic bondage to God. I witness to this testimony of the saints.

I invite you now to a very complex discipleship to Jesus Christ, one part of which is best understood as slavery to his God and the obligations entailed. As disciples we shall stand out as peculiar in our devotion to the duty of elementary generosity. When those to whom generosity is directed fail to benefit, and our patience runs thin, and money runs out, and generosity means hardship for us, we shall remember the extent of the obedience of Jesus Christ the slave, obedient unto death. I invite you also to become a lover of God, to take on that slavery with a glad heart, and to rise to a vision of God's glory. The loveliness of the Creator, the divine freedom to which we are drawn, makes that slavery bliss. Amen.

This was my sermon for Robert Thornburg's birthday that was preached at Marsh Chapel on October 8, 1995.

20. GOD AND THE WEALTHY: LOST AND FOUND

Read and reflect on Job 23:1-9, 16-17; Psalm 22:1-15; Hebrews 4:12-16; Mark 10:17-31.

Once again I have the pleasure to occupy the Marsh Chapel pulpit on this Sunday of the year, which is the birthday weekend of Dean Robert Thornburg and his twin brother, Richard. If this is becoming a tradition, which I hope it is, my only fear is that the Dean will associate me with the accumulation of birthdays. As he mentioned last Sunday, however, this past year he has triumphed over some health problems, and so he should recognize birthdays to be occasions for rejoicing. There is an apt Chinese aphorism on a birthday card for this: "Birthdays are good for you, those who have most live longest." Once attributed to Kung Fu Tzu, or Confucius, that line is now traced by most scholars to his entrepreneurial cousin, Hall Mark Tzu. Our lectionary texts for today are a bit more complicated.

We have two characters to reflect on today, Job and the rich man who Mark reports came to Jesus and who Matthew (19:16-34) describes as young. Their stories come from quite different parts of the Bible and are described in different scales. Job's story has an epic sweep, of which our text for today is but a small part. It begins and ends in the symbolic structure of the heavenly court. Job's own home is a world of vast pastures and busy foreign trade, and God comes to meet him in a whirlwind. The Young Man, by contrast, is mentioned in only this short story, which is repeated in Matthew and Luke (18:18-30). Instead of a heavenly court there is only the band of disciples trying to figure out what righteousness is. The Young Man's world is Jesus' confused Palestine; and there being no whirlwind, he simply walks away at the end to be heard of no more in Scripture by any explicit identification.

Despite these differences, the two characters have much in common. For instance both of them are righteous, certifiably so and without irony or qualification. Job's afflictions came, you remember, because Satan wagered with God that Job was righteous only because righteousness pays and that Job would curse God when righteousness did not bring gratification. So Satan destroyed Job's economic empire, killed all his children and servants, left him only his wife who was a nag, and then afflicted him with a loathsome painful disease. On behalf of Job's wife, it should be noted that she too lost her fortune and her children and gained an invalid for a husband; we can understand her response, which was to curse Job's integrity and God. Through all this Job suffered but would not curse God. "The Lord gave and the Lord has taken away: blessed be the name of the Lord," Job said. "Shall we receive the good from the hand of the Lord," he asked his wife, "and not the bad?" Those are powerful testimonies for our time. When the stock market crashed in 1929 and people lost their fortunes, grown men in despair cast themselves down from tall buildings. When your children die, all pieties seem out of place. When we suffer from chronic, painful, debilitating, and socially disgusting diseases, who of us can keep our minds straight and not capitulate with self-pity and blame? Job's wife is a typical modern American. Yet Job was steadfast in honoring God through all his suffering.

Mark's Young Man was similar to Job though not depicted in such a heroic way. When he came to Jesus, asking what he might do to enter the kingdom of God, Jesus asked him about the Ten Commandments having to do with other people, and he said he had obeyed them since his youth. Jesus believed him without further question.

Job and the Young Man were also alike in being loved by God. Job's troubles began because God was bragging on him in the mythic heavenly court; and at the end God restored Job's fortune, family, and health. God's love for the Young Man—that is, Jesus' love for him—is more poignant and believable in a human scale. Luke identifies the man as a young aristocrat and yet he runs up to Jesus full of zeal for God's kingdom, falls to his knees, and asks Jesus, What more? Questioning shows him righteous according to the law; and you can imagine how difficult that was in those days when the Romans traduced the aristocracy, especially the rich members of the ruling class. He was thoroughly winsome, and Jesus' heart went out to him. The disciples obviously saw Jesus' love for the Young Man and envied it because they immediately pointed out that they had done what he could not do, give up everything to follow Jesus. Not that they had all that much to give up. Both Job and the Young Man were righteous, lovable, and beloved.

Given these characteristics, what is there in Job and the Young Man with which we can identify? Few of us are rich, few if any even believe ourselves to be righteous, let alone have that belief stand up under test. Even the most winsome of us have our bad moments, and our common desperate passion to be loved signals a deep anxiety that no one really cares. But we have more in common with Job and the Young Man than you might think.

You don't have to be the "greatest man in the East," as Job was called, to despair and curse God when you lose your job and home. More than a few in this city are unemployed, homeless, and without prospects. Rich or poor, our children die from diseases we cannot cure, from accidents we cannot prevent, from violence in school, from the death-wish of drugs. Many among us are afflicted with diseases that cause pain, that cripple, that make us loathsome, that destroy hope for the future. Most of us so pained and suffering look to God for magic and, when it doesn't come, curse God in despair beneath the breath, beneath awareness, beneath fulsome piety.

Nor do you have to be a rich aristocrat to have the Young Man's ego, his sense of place, and expectation. Few of us inherit social status and power; what we have, however humble, is largely earned. How can we give that up when Jesus calls? Families are not always perfect, but they give us a place; furthermore, we know it takes work to maintain a family, work to raise children, work to win respect from parents and kin, work to order the home as a nurturing context for celebrating life's joys and griefs in perspective. How can we walk away from that work to follow Jesus? Most of us would be like the Rich Young Man. Only those who have nothing, and therefore give up nothing, can turn around to follow Jesus easily; and unless they quickly acquire the wealth of Christian living, which looks for all the world like crucifixion, they will wander away down the very next enticing path that promises without demanding. Most of us do have many things to lose in fortune, family, and health; do lose it from time to time; lack Job's patience; but like the Young Man cannot abandon the ego's commitments. And about this, hear the text from Hebrews:

> "Indeed, the word of God is living and active, sharper than any two-edged sword, piercing until it divides soul from spirit, joints from marrow; it is able to judge the thoughts and intentions of the heart. And before him no creature is hidden, but all are naked and laid bare to the eyes of the one to whom we must render an account." (4:12-13)

136

These are stories about us. Our struggles and sufferings make us vulnerable to the living and active word of God. After all our excuses and explanations, after all our complaints about unfair fate, unhelpful partners, small support, uneven odds, unreal expectations, untimeliness, pressure, stress, and Why me? when the blind indifferent cosmic causes trample our fortune, our family, or our health, we are still under judgment and cannot hide. Sharper than any two-edged sword, piercing until it divides soul from spirit, joints from marrow, the Word of God puts into judgment the thoughts and intentions of our hearts—more in times of stress than in ease.

Job and the Young Man are alike in one more respect: They went searching for God. Job in our text sought God to demand an accounting, to explain himself, and to persuade God his suffering was unjustified. And with those purposes God could not be found. Like Job we too seek God sometimes in order to put a moral frame around suffering. If only we could understand our suffering as deserved because of some unknown sin, or better, as a mistake in cosmic reckoning, or as a consequence of someone else's guilt, then at least it would make sense. But suffering usually does not make sense, and God refuses to be found as a moral person who sends good and bad for cause.

The Young Man sought God out of the flush of enthusiastic virtue. He was well placed, he was rich, he had kept the commandments, and he must have sensed that he was very close to inheriting eternal life. With winsome goodwill he ran to Jesus for the crowning touch, almost humble and hopeful; and Jesus laid him naked and bare. "Why call me good? No one is good but God alone." As if to say, when you come to God to use divinity for your own purposes, even purposes of salvation, God will step back from persona to persona. As if to ask, when only God is good and Jesus is not, what are you asking for yourself?

And then, through love and hope Jesus saw the one thing that was indeed needed—if only the Young Man could leave behind the rich things that propped up his identity, he could be God's own innocent, entering the kingdom like one of the children of whom Jesus had been speaking when he ran up (Mark 10:13-16). Like a two-edged sword Jesus' words pierced to his heart, separated soul and spirit, joints from marrow; and the Young Man left a different person: naked and bare. He knew ever after he could not have his rich self and heaven too. We do not know what happened to him afterward. Surely Jesus longed for him to turn back and come with him. We'd like to think perhaps the Young Man was Lazarus of

John's Gospel, or Joseph of Arimathea, or the young man who was with Jesus when the soldiers came for him in Gethsemane as recounted later in Mark's Gospel (Mark 14:15-52). But we do not know, and the rest of that man's story is not our story.

Here is the moral of both stories, Job's and the Young Man's: When we pursue God to secure some account, some redress, or some blessing, God recedes and we are left with only our selfish projections of God satisfying us, evanescent plays of our ego's imagination on a rocky surface. But remember what happened to Job: He did not find God; but God came to him in a whirlwind, revealed the divine glory, and gave Job the perspective from which to see exactly why he should bless God for life's sufferings as well as satisfactions. We can cast into the whirlwind the fanciful heavenly court and the anthropomorphic wagering of God and Satan as well as Job's moral vindication. Come what may, good or bad, God the creator hides glory and fulfillment in all that comes. That is not what we want to discover when we insist God conform to our hopes, but it is what God reveals; and God does come in whirlwinds to take us up past sufferings and satisfactions to glory.

In the case of the Young Man, the disciples offered themselves as ones who had abandoned all for Jesus, but Jesus returned without that distraction to the Young Man. Hard though it be to enter the kingdom of God when your possessions give you an ego that you think God ought to want to save, nevertheless, "for God, all things are possible." God sets free the rich and those of us whose very modest riches still entangle us. The Young Man approached Jesus to get something; and Jesus said, You do not need more, not even what you have: just follow me. His problem was not with riches but with attachments. People can damn themselves by attachments to poverty, to dysfunctional families, to their diseases as well as to wealth, children, and health.

My friends, I invite you to the freedom of God's kingdom which you can find by turning to Jesus. Become his disciple and take on his ministry. Where people are hungry, feed them. Where they are homeless, help them. Where they are in prison, befriend them. Where their hunger and poverty and criminal wickedness come from the condition of society, change it. Where conditions are unjust, speak out. Where people are exploited, change the system. Where people oppress with violence, bring peace. Where people rage with violence, bring peace. Where people want God to fix them, teach them to help themselves. Where people blame others, the gods, or God, recite them one of Christ's double-bladed parables.

Where you want to blame others, ask what you can do yourself. Where you suffer poverty, loss, or pain, practice Job's patience. Where you long for comfort, seek Christ in strange people. Where you pant for salvation like the beast at the water brook, give up that ambition and follow God's spirit.

For God is in the whirlwind and the fire, the deep water and the small voice. God is in the knife-edge that shaves our soul from spirit and separates joints from marrow—in our worst sins, in our worst fears, in our worst weakness, in our worst failures, in our worst pride, in our worst bluffs, in our worst hatred of self and condemnation of conscience, God is there loving us like Jesus looking at that Young Man. You can escape your pain, your ego, and your conscience by sleep, drugs, and sex; but you cannot escape God loving you and tugging your heart. When your people are oppressed, God loves them to new power. When your people are oppressors, God loves them to repentance. When you are wrong, God loves you anyway. When you tire, God loves you in weakness. When you are dead, God loves us to life. When you are mortally attached and bound to death, you are even then God's beloved. When finally in glory God gives you indifference to riches and pain, you can love God with the bliss that fulfills salvation.

> For I am convinced that neither death, nor life, nor angels, nor rulers, nor things present, nor things to come, nor powers, nor height, nor depth, nor loss of fortune, nor death of family, nor disease, nor arrogance, nor small visions of God, nor large visions of self, nor fear of weakness, nor refusal to abandon oneself to God, nor anything else in all creation, will be able to separate us from the love of God in Christ Jesus our Lord. (elaborated from Romans 8:38-39)

The love of God was in Jesus' eye when he looked at the earnest young man. It is here in our shaky hands. I invite you to the love that is itself, finally in glory, indifferent to our demands and failures alike and that transforms us into lovers of God, the most wondrous of all fortunes, like Job's, who blessed God in all things. Amen.

This was preached a year before the previous one, on October 9, 1994, also in recognition of Robert Thornburg's birthday, in Marsh Chapel at Boston University.

21. GROWING STRONG FOR FALSEHOOD, NOT FOR TRUTH

Read and reflect on Jeremiah 9:1-6, 31:31-37.

Most of the book of Jeremiah is filled with complaints, warnings and lamentations. The word *Jeremiad* in English means a prolonged lamentation or complaint, for good reason. There is a brief intense hiatus from the thirtieth through the thirty-third chapters in which Jeremiah speaks a consoling word and promises a new covenant; the second part of our text this morning is from that section. But the warnings and complaints resume in chapter 34 and continue to the end in chapter 52, with only occasional references to God's restorative intentions and powers.

The main framing complaint of Jeremiah had to do with politics and international relations, with misguided alliances with great powers, and the like. But with forty-nine chapters of complaints, Jeremiah touched on about every complaint possible. I want to lift up for your consideration the complaint in chapter 9 about falsehood and truth: "They bend their tongues like bows; they have grown strong in the land for falsehood, and not for truth." A little later in the chapter Jeremiah returns to the military metaphor from another side: "Their tongue is a deadly arrow; it speaks deceit through the mouth" (9:8). Whether as bow or as arrow, the tongue is a death-dealing weapon.

Jeremiah's preoccupation with weaponry is understandable in light of the repeated defeats Israel and Judah had suffered at the hands of the superpowers. The fertile valleys were filled with corpses. "We look for peace, but find no good; for a time of healing, but there is terror instead" (14:19). Jeremiah's concern with falsehood is not limited to diplomatic treachery and fawning attempts to curry favor with various kings and warlords, although there was enough of that. Rather, falsehood had become a way of ordinary life. "Beware of your neighbors," wrote Jeremiah, "and put no trust in any of your kin; for all your kin are supplanters, and every neighbor goes around like a slanderer. They all deceive their neighbors, and no one speaks the truth; they have taught their tongues to speak lies; they commit iniquity and are too weary to repent. Oppression upon oppression, deceit upon deceit! They refuse to know me, says the LORD" (9:4-6).

What kind of falsehood oppresses and kills like an arrow? Not simple mistakes, or even greedy deceptions that people know to guard against. The falsehoods that deal death are cloaked in righteousness. To attack a falsehood slathered in righteousness seems to be attacking righteousness itself. And of course the arrow deals its death to the applause of all who see only the righteous covering and not the false weapon beneath.

The most common form of this falsehood in ordinary life is the malicious gossip cultivated by people who believe that their way of life is very virtuous and is under attack by someone's alleged behavior. Paul, in the first chapter of Romans, saw gossip as the direct result of worshiping creatures rather than God, and lists it along with murder, slander, and God-hating. I never understood why gossip was important enough to be included in the list until I realized that what he meant by gossip was not merely comparing notes about people's private lives but doing so in a way that results in their being isolated, demeaned, and destroyed.

The key to the power of falsehood is its righteous covering. You know how gossip gets started in church. A person is talking on the phone with her friend about the church bazaar when she smells the burning giblets on the stove. She quickly excuses herself from the phone conversation, but that is reported to a third person as having been abrupt. The fourth person hears that she was insulting to her phone partner, and the fifth person hears that she thinks the church bazaar is a stupid waste of time. The sixth person hears that she thinks the church is a stupid waste of time, and the seventh hears that she is leaving the church. The eighth finally is given to believe that the only reason she would leave the church after all these years is that she has been having an affair with the pastor, which has just been discovered. In all of this there is a provoking incident—the quick termination of the phone conversation—imperfectly understood and misinterpreted through the righteousness of friendship and church. And no one of the gossips is responsible for a big mistake.

Or consider the businessman who takes his wife to lunch, puts it on the company expense account, and is caught by the bookkeeper. He is reprimanded by the boss and has to pay back the money. The bookkeeper tells a visiting salesman that he fudged his expense slip, and the salesman tells his friends at the bar that the man was caught attempting to embezzle funds. From that conversation the word goes out to the competing companies that he did embezzle funds, and they pass the word that he should not be employed by any of the competitors. The president of one of those companies then tells the man's boss that he is unemployable because of a history of embezzlement, the boss fires him, and he is unemployable forever. A small incident of wrongdoing, though a common practice, is falsely reputed to be a habit of great evil that costs the man his livelihood. The story is distorted by the ethos of righteousness in business, a point about which many of the actors feel secretly guilty. And yet no one is responsible for the whole lie.

In our own time and closer to home, we have a new righteousness, that of the victim role. Please do not misunderstand my point. There are real victims in this world, children who are victims of incest and violence, persons who are victims of sexual harassment, abuse, and rape. This is a violent society, as Jeremiah would remind us, with plentiful semiautomatic repeating bows and arrows; people here respond to frustration quickly with violence. Women legitimately worry about their safety and men do too, if secretly. Children should be protected by the state from abusive adults.

But the proper response to being a victim is first to own the fact and its pain, to express appropriate anger; and then to reject the victim role. Face the violation that has been done to you and do not let that stop you from full life. Full life, the life to which Christians are called in the resurrected Christ, rides on the courage to go forward. To engage life almost inevitably is to get hurt in love, to get hurt in sports, to get hurt in intellectual ambitions, to have downs as well as ups to your career, to be hurt by your children, to be hurt by your friends, and to have many dark nights of the soul. But don't avoid relationships because you might get hurt again. Don't stay home because you might get hurt outside. Don't settle for ignorance because enlightenment is upsetting. Don't pick an unchallenging career because you might fail. Don't be emotionally frigid because those you risk to love might hurt you. Don't let your soul drift because a deliberate search for God might be lonely. To be victimized is to be hurt by others, and sometimes that hurt takes a long time to heal. But to accept the victim's role forever, not just the fact and consequences of victimization but the role, to think yourself into the victim identity as your only identity, is to oppress yourself, and the result of that oppression is false righteousness.

The most common example of this kind of death-dealing falsehood results from our heightened sensitivity to sexual harassment and abuse. There are many, too many, genuine instances of clear-cut prolonged sexual harassment; and there are far too many cases of violent rape or date-rape where women are coerced by those whom they thought trustworthy. But romantic dalliance is notoriously filled with ambiguous signals and misinterpreted cues. One person's yes is another person's no. In some circumstances a yes does mean no, and a no means yes. And sexual incidents mean different things to different people, a commitment of undying love to one person, a frivolity to another; merely unsatisfying to one person, date-rape to another. All the advice these days to be clear and unambiguous is well taken indeed, but the hope for total unambiguity is vain.

I have seen ministers, faculty, staff members, and students utterly ruined by gossip that builds upon ambiguous or small incidents, incidents that might have great private meaning for those directly involved but that are given larger public significance through gossip. The incident might be a genuine case of unwanted harassment; it might be a case of forced sexual activity. Or the incident might begin with mixed signals, with the woman wanting to say no but the man not getting the message, with the woman feeling deeply hurt and the man realizing only after the fact that he had been rejected. In any of these cases, feelings strong enough to require expression in the community ought first be framed as a complaint to the community authorities so that the rights of all can be protected against uncontrollable gossip. Human rights are destroyed by gossip just as much as by physical torture. In an educational institution like ours or a church denomination or a business company, a direct complaint can initiate a procedure that ascertains facts, clarifies the meanings of the signals and the intentions, secures understanding and apology and fixes remedies where possible. If the facts indicate that a crime might have been committed, the procedures facilitate the aggrieved party in making a formal legal complaint with criminal proceedings to follow.

Yet even where the institution's procedures settle the matter, with the parties agreeing that the incident is terminated and no legal action is pressed, the situation is ripe for gossip if the lovers of righteous falsehood are about. The women in the neighborhood begin to talk about the accused man as if he were a dangerous specimen, and the men shun him because they don't want to be associated with someone identified as what all men are secretly feared to be. He walks down the street and conversation around him stops because it had been about him. He is personally isolated and publicly scapegoated for all the sexual abuse women have suffered, for all they remember or imagine, for all they fear about men and for all that men fear that women say about them. And the aggrieved woman too, no matter how innocent she might be, comes to be known as a complainer, not to be trusted, a reputation all the more hurtful the more the community knows deep down that rumor has lost its touch with fact and become fastened to fears.

As I say, I've seen that happen to ministers, to faculty and staff, and to students. The righteousness of opposing sexual abuse and of being the potential victim of such abuse can cover a poisoned arrow that deals death to individuals and ruins entire communities. No one has responsibility for the whole falsehood, and everyone thinks they are protecting future victims as well as exacting divine justice. Yet the falsehood is deep and deadly, poisoning the community as it destroys individuals.

Jeremiah says we have "grown strong in the land for falsehood, and not for truth." Our strength in falsehood is nowhere better illustrated than in the propensity to spin a web of gossip around individuals, objectifying them, isolating them, scapegoating them, representing them as the perpetrator of all evil deeds feared, and congratulating ourselves on great righteousness because of opposition to the oppressor.

Against this falsehood we must grow strong in these truths: with respect to gossip, most of the time it is none of our business; with respect to gossip, most of the time it has the facts wrong; with respect to gossip, most of the time the motivation stems from bad experience and special interests for which the victim is only an accidental symbol; with respect to gossip, no individual is in the position to take responsibility for balanced truth and the prevention of exaggeration, and so all are culpable of a sin for which no one has the power to be responsible. Listen to Jeremiah: Make our land strong in the truth, and not falsehood.

Compassionate forgiveness is the heart of the Christian gospel. Compassionate forgiveness of ourselves allows us to live with our own propensity to gossip, to acknowledge it and put it aside. Compassionate forgiveness of those who are victims of abuse is deeply needed to help them accept themselves despite their bruises, despite the anger they may have directed against themselves, and despite their own guilts. Compassionate forgiveness of those accused of abuse, after appropriate righteous anger and the location of justice, is even more deeply needed, all the more where the accusation is valid. We must be careful not to forgive someone with fanfare of sins constructed by the rumor mill rather than those of fact. Nothing could be more offensive. But we must communicate to the accused God's compassionate forgiveness for sin whatever its truth and evil. It was for the sinners, after all, not the healthy and righteous, that Christ came. Where you see people objectified by gossip, isolated, ridiculed as different, and held up as dangerous bogeymen, take them by the hand and bring them into your group of forgiven sinners.

Jeremiah not only complained but also promised the new covenant in which God's law is written in our hearts. We will not have to be taught about God because we will know God already. Have you any idea how *disconsoling* this is to a Christian preacher who believes we now live in the new covenant? Are not we, strong in falsehood, more like the deceiving oppressors in Jeremiah's complaint? "Oppression upon oppression, deceit upon deceit! They refuse to know me, says the LORD." Can we take some comfort from Jeremiah? Why, we may ask him, are we supposed to know God, now in the New Covenant? Jeremiah said, "they shall all know me, from the least of them to the greatest, says the LORD; for I will forgive their iniquity, and remember their sin no more."

My Christian friends, let me remind you of what you already know, that God knows your sins and forgives them. God knows the wickedness of your heart and still finds you lovely. God knows us to be a people with a victim mentality but says get up and walk—our sins are not remembered. God knows we are a community of backbiting and defensive gossips but says that is forgiven—tell the truth now. God knows our sinful society oppresses and abuses but says those iniquities are forgiven—from now on live justly. God knows many suffer from illness, poverty, oppression, and abuse and says that is the essence of the divine life lived with joy and grace—after crucifixion comes resurrection.

The New Covenant is the cosmic drama in which we are too slow to wake up to our roles. God loves us with a zest that turns our hearts on fire. That love forgives all sins and makes us shine as beloved people. We know that. How can we remember it? By our own constant practice of love and forgiveness, and only by that. When we do not love and forgive, we sink into forgetfulness of God's love. When we accuse others of evil and primp in our own righteousness, we forget what we know of God whose law is written in our hearts. Therefore practice forgiving even as you are forgiven, for forgiveness begins with God's forgiveness of yourself that you must respect. Practice discernment of good and evil so as to know what to praise and what to challenge, change, and forgive. Practice finding sinners and showing them forgiveness. Practice loving our friends in respect to and despite their sins. Practice finding the outcasts and bringing them in. Practice befriending the lonely and despised. Practice your contributions to a community of forgiven sinners. Practice forgiving even as you are forgiven: practice, practice, practice, and you will remember God whose love is already written in your heart. Amen.

This is another sermon preached in the context of the introductory Hebrew Bible course in the Boston University School of Theology. The text assigned me by Professor Katheryn Pfisterer Darr was Jeremiah.

22. Tests for People and Gods

Read and reflect on Psalm 66:8-20, Acts 17:22-28.

To the 1993 graduates of Boston University the pulpit of Marsh Chapel extends happy congratulations. With their parents, friends, and families, the faculty heaves a great sigh of thanksgiving and wonder: there were times when this day seemed in doubt to some. To friends and family, I express on behalf of the graduates a profound gratitude that will grow as the years pass. Again to the graduates I want to say that far beyond the help from faculty, classmates, and family, yours is an education that you have earned and taken for yourselves, your responsibility, your first major creation.

The preacher in this place last year was Fred Rogers, Mr. Rogers. He received a hero's welcome here and at commencement. The young man sitting next to me during this service said, "Mr. Rogers was the only one who understood me when I was five." The amazing grace of that day was that Fred Rogers was a hero of gentleness when all the other heroes of the generation were competitive athletes, singers of sex and violence, movie stars with automatic rifles, or victorious soldiers with smart bombs. The grace of Mr. Rogers passed through Schwarzenegger and Schwarzkopf like Israel through the Red Sea, which gives me great hope for this generation and the confidence to preach this sermon. For I have an edge to lay on Mr. Rogers' advice for surviving the trials of childhood.

American society has slowly come to realize that the slogan "I'm OK, you're OK" is false and dangerous. I'm not OK. I dare not presume to speak for you, but surely all those others out there are not OK. And perhaps the gods we serve are not OK, at least as we choose to serve them. So we need the personal and social trials by fire and water; as the psalmist said, and as Paul said, we need to ask whether our gods are true. The trials are hard, the stakes are high, and the measure of our generation depends on how well we pass through them. That's the bad news when you all thought you had taken your last exam.

The "I'm OK, you're OK" attitude arose from some good motives. One was Mr. Rogers' own philosophy that understanding things is good and that denial is bad. With an increased understanding and generosity of perspective, many of the things that seem threatening to the childish and ignorant turn out to be OK. So far, Mr. Rogers' message is the university's philosophy expressed for children: look outward, look inward, and understand.

Another decent motive for the "I'm OK, you're OK" attitude was a reaction to the cumulative discovery of bigotry in America. The civil rights movement of the 1950s and 1960s revealed many kinds and places of racism that only African Americans knew about before. We came to recognize anti-Semitism at home. The movements for the rights of women and many minorities have shown how common stereotypes falsely depict people as wrongly limited or harmful—stereotypes the acceptance of which deprives people of their legitimate opportunities and rights and subjects them to undeserved calumny. In the face of bigotry, "I'm OK, you're OK" can mean "I am confident about approaching you with curiosity and care, and accept your differences until given a good reason not to." For the American nation of minorities defending themselves in a competitive environment, "I'm OK, you're OK" can mean a step beyond bigotry toward the half of Jesus' Great Commandment that consists in loving your neighbor.

Nevertheless, admitting this much good in the matter, the attitude toward life framed by "I'm OK, you're OK" is deeply false. *Ethnic cleansing* is not merely a different process of social arrangement: It is wicked, wicked, wicked, and it was wicked when the Nazis did it to the Jews, Gypsies, and homosexuals; it was wicked when the Turks did it to the Armenians, when the Chinese did it to the Muslims, and when the European-Americans did it to the native peoples here. The Somalian reign of warlords is not merely a different polity but a wicked abuse of government leading to what Thomas Hobbes called a constant disposition to war: "In such condition," Hobbes said

> There is no place for Industry, because the fruit thereof is uncertain; and consequently no Culture of the Earth, no Navigation, nor use of the

commodities that may be imported by Sea; no commodious Building; no Instruments of moving, and removing such things as require much force; no Knowledge of the face of the Earth; no account of Time; no Arts; no Letters; no Society; and which is worst of all, continuall feare, and danger of violent death; And the life of man, solitary, poore, nasty, brutish, and short. (*Leviathan* I, Chapter XIII, 104)

Ethnic cleansing and the chaos of warlords are human conditions often supported by people who have good intentions and righteous, if aggrieved, memories. Let me ask you: In the right circumstances don't you fear we ourselves might support those wicked conditions? We of course would not do it on purpose but would stumble into it stupidly while pursuing our own benign interests. Before we know it, we would have to cover our mistakes by defending what amounts to disguised commitments to ethnic cleansing or to a weak justice that serves our interests. Then our racial, sexual, and class prejudices would have become necessary policies to which we are committed without admitting it. Of course we would not deliberately extend these prejudices and rationalizations to actual wickedness. In fact we good people often draw clear lines: We may exaggerate so far but not cross the line to lie; we may compete hard but not cross the line to cheat; we may press our advantage but not cross the line to exploit; we may defend ourselves from attack but not cross the line to violence and murder. Then suddenly the line is behind us; we already have crossed over and are liars, cheaters, exploiters, and complicit in systems of murderous violence. This is the way sin works, my friends, and it is the reason I, at least, am not OK. Who has not crossed lines like these?

You know now why the trials through fire and water are so precious. When like stupid sheep we crop our way through some green pasture, head down and blind to the dangers to our souls and people, pray that life will ignite a fire to wake us up. Hope to be tested, smelted, refined like silver. When we are backed into prejudice and rationalization because we benefit from local forms of ethnic cleansing or weak justice, pray for a flood to drown our sins and make us swim, to make us build an ark for our sisters and brothers. When we draw the lines of sin and then cross them, pray for the fire of God and the waters of new life. Pray for the divine fire to show us the truth and burn our illusions, to temper us with despair and present us unadorned, to displace our blindness with God's light, our excuses with God's truth, our sins with God's glory. Pray for the water of life to wash our evil and self-hatred, to kill off the worthless self and give birth to righteousness, to carry us back to the waters of creation where, by God's spirit and word, we and the world are made new. Lord, try us by fire and water that we might stand this side of evil and sin no more.

We hardly need to pray for trials. The human condition is generous with afflictions, enemies, firestorms, and floods. By no means do I advocate that we look upon gratuitous suffering as a good thing. Afflictions are blind with respect to morality and beset the innocent as much as the guilty. Rather, I am adding to Mr. Rogers' generous recipe for the improvement of the human condition through understanding a religious view of the importance of trials for coping with the evil side of our nature and society.

The greatest trial, of course, is the directly religious one. What god do we serve? This was Paul's question to the Athenians when he saw they hedged their bets on the traditional pantheon by honoring the unknown God. Paul was not questioning whether they believed, but in what they believed. Important as the question of belief or faith is, it is not the relevant question to ask when hunting for the right god, or when testing the god we worship to see whether that is the true God. The right question here is not about faith but about theology.

Theological questions are neither merely private nor only academic. The Hindus whose slogan is *Shanti, Shanti, Shanti*—Peace, Peace, Peace— are caught in a deep perversion of their theology when in the name of their religion they attack Muslims in India or Buddhists in Sri Lanka. The Protestants and Catholics, who serve the Lord of love, are caught in a deep perversion of their theology when in the name of their religion they attack one another in Ireland. David Koresh and the Branch Davidians were not crazy and they did not commit suicide—those are misplaced categories: their self-immolation was a positive affirmation of life triumphant in the face of persecution as understood by a desperately mistaken theology. Theology is of great public moment.

If the god we serve in our hearts is money or power or success, we are theologically mistaken and can harm others as well as ourselves. If the god we serve in our hearts is pleasure or sex or beauty or knowledge, there is hope that the true God might be present; but the theology is still idolatrous. If the god we serve says we and the lives we lead are OK, our theology is blind. If the god we serve promises a quick fix without demanding a new life, our theology is self-serving. If the god we serve is a part of the world but not its creator, our theology is too small. If the god we serve dwells in temples and needs our sacrifices, our theology is too human. If the god we serve is closer to us than to other peoples, our theology is too biased. If the god we serve is strange and inaccessible, then our theology keeps us from the God in whom "we live and move and have our being" (Acts 17:28). Our greatest trial is not speaking without lies, not struggling without cheating, not pressing advantage without exploiting, not securing ourselves without violence. Our greatest trial is the theological test of finding the true God.

Now I realize this is a heavy message for a family day of celebration, but it is the only message, really, that comes from the University pulpit. I realize also that talk about "finding God" is a little too religious, even too syrupy, because most of us have at least half our heart in the secular world. So let me put the point another way.

My friends who are graduating, your university education should give you knowledge and skills with the wisdom to understand their true context. So you should now be able to earn money, exercise power, and enjoy success without harming yourselves or others; if so, you have put those things in divine context. You should be able to take pleasure, delight in sex, love beauty, and enlarge your soul in knowledge without idolatry; if so, your schooling has put these things in divine context. You should be able to act in the world with capacity and courage and without the delusions that I'm OK or you're OK. You should expect no quick fixes but hard work accompanied by constant reformations of character. You should see the world in all its multifarious detail and contingent upon its creator who is not a magic meddler. You should be ready to worship with true piety, not mistaking temples for divinity or self-righteousness for divine service. You should assume that God is as close to others as to ourselves, and for that reason we are all as close as brothers and sisters. You should see that we do not live and move and have our being in ourselves, or even with one another only, but also as the offspring of the immense and eternal Creator. If you can do these things, your education has brought you to what Paul and I mean by the true God.

The personal test of the true God for whom we go through trials of fire and water comes at those lines that mark the edges of sin. When you cross the line from exaggeration to lies, does your God confront you on the other side with truth and also the power to be truthful again? When you cross from competing to cheating, does your God confront you with honesty and also the power of repentance? When you cross from pressing advantage to exploitation, does your God confront you with justice and also reconciliation? When you cross from defending security to complicity in murderous violence, does your God confront you with judgment and also new life?

If your answer is yes, you are blessed and you also get an A in theology. If your answer is no, there are two possibilities. Your theology is bad and needs work. Or you have never met someone who conveyed to you the overwhelming divine love that frees you to see yourself as in a mirror face to face and accept the grace to head on toward perfection from wherever you are.

This brings my message back to Mr. Rogers, the symbol for a generation of the gentleness that enables children to understand their fears and wickedness and still to grow up toward perfection. My prayer for you graduates is that your education here has taken something of the power into which Mr. Rogers taps for children. May your eyes and hearts be open to the true divine context. May you find the love that brings both true judgment and renewing grace, and pass it on to our blind and halt world. May you bind yourselves to our time and live in it fully, rejoicing that our time lies in the divine eternity. Remember us with favor and pass on our love. Amen.

Most of my bureaucratic sermons are addressed to the School of Theology. The Baccalaureate Service, however, which is part of the Commencement ceremonies at Boston University, begins the festive day in Marsh Chapel, involves the President and Provost of the University, and is well attended by students and families from all schools. It is Christian in its origins, but addresses an audience drawn from all faiths and anti-faiths represented in our large university. The challenge is to put the gospel in terms of "public theology." This is the baccalaureate sermon from May 16, 1993.

23. WIND OR WINE? TESTING THE SPIRITS OF OUR TIME

Read and reflect on Numbers 11:24-30, Acts 2:1-17.

The Baccalaureate Service on the eve of commencement is not a propitious time to use the symbols of wind and wine in their biblical senses. Wind is what you have had enough of, coming from your professors. Wine is the object of your longing for later tonight, and Peter's knock-down argument that his people could not be drunk because it is only 9 A.M. might not seem so persuasive tomorrow morning.

But for the moment I want to call your attention to the less immediate but deeper potencies of these symbols. Wind is the Spirit of God that was present at the creation, in the account at the beginning of Genesis. You will remember that the windy spirit of God was timelessly roiling the primeval waters into a chaos that bore no forms until the Speech of God made things with a difference, light from darkness, land from sea, night into day. The same trio of divine wind, water, and speech was present at Jesus' baptism, referring that moment to the original core of creation. Elijah the prophet received the divine Spirit as wind, as the still small voice, and as the fire that lit the altars and burned over the priests of Baal. So when Luke lifts up the wind in describing the sudden transformative presence of God in his story of Pentecost, he is sounding two themes like sympathetic vibrations. One is that the event he was recounting was itself a function of the same creative power that makes all things new. The other is that the transformation of wind into fire has a moral impulse that sets righteousness over against evil. So much for the resonances of wind.

As for wine, Luke develops that negative symbol as a denial of the very legitimacy of the nascent Christian movement. The pivotal significance of

153

the Pentecost event was the translation of the gospel of Jesus the Galilean into the languages and circumstances of diverse peoples from around the world. The Spirit did not produce babel but translations, and the local gospel was made relevant to circumstances Jesus and his rude disciples could not imagine. Christianity exists only in translation, not in Galilean cultural dogmatism, not in a universally neutral abstraction, but in translations that bring judgment, redemption, and new life across a world of many cultures. Pentecost is the event that symbolizes with wind and fire the coming into being of the cross-cultural renewing power claimed for the Christian movement.

But of course the big-city Jerusalem skeptics thought all those languages were babel and that the Christians were drunk. The skeptical counterparts today might say that they were carried away emotionally, or that their religious claims were wish-fulfilling fictions, or that they were drunk. For Luke, Pentecost meant the victory of God's renewing power over the dispersion of languages at the tower of Babel, not by returning them to one language but by translating through all languages with the gospel of salvation. If instead the Christians were drunk, it would have been like Noah who, after bringing his family and specimens of all living creatures through the trials of the flood, got drunk and ruined the pristine new beginning God had planned.

For those planning to celebrate later I should say that the Bible does not have only bad things to say about wine. Psalm 104 lists it with staples of good things from God:

> You cause the grass to grow for the cattle,
>   and plants for people to use,
> to bring forth food from the earth,
>   and wine to gladden the human heart,
> oil to make the face shine,
>   and bread to strengthen the human heart.
>   (14-15)

So it is all right to celebrate tonight as long as you keep the Psalms constantly on your lips.

When you recover from your celebrations tomorrow you will discover yourself in a world filled with spirits. Some of those spirits will be divine like Luke's tongues of fire. Others will be just intoxicants. And the great challenge for your generation will be to distinguish the two, to support the divine spirits bearing creativity and renewal, and to limit the intoxicating spirits to moderation at parties. This is my big message: The challenge of your generation is theological—you must be able to tell the true spirits from the false, and the civilizations of the world depend upon you for that, for you are their educated leaders.

Ours is a time a little like Noah's after the flood or like the first century around the Mediterranean when the Roman Empire had interrupted all local cultures: There is a vacuum in political and social life. The old habits are weakened and largely irrelevant. Whatever happens will be a new creation, and the question is whether it will be good like a divine creation or vapid and filled with suffering like a terminal hangover.

The cold war has been exhausted, and the vacuum left in power politics has been filled not with the flowering of the democratic spirit but by ancient hatreds and religious wars. Governments around the world now recognize the global character of economic interdependencies but have not found ways to protect local populations from devastating international shifts of wealth and jobs. Americans have learned from a generation of moral and political prophets about the evils of racism, sexism, and bigoted prejudice against minorities but have been left with an empty relativism that says no life is better than another or even much better than nothing. Our science is hastily conquering disease and removing obstacles to human ambition but may be turning our planet into a Sahara fit only for roaches and rats' bones. In your generation human beings will begin exploring and colonizing places far beyond earth, and yet we do not know whether those plantations across the Milky Way will be like extended translations of God's good news or merely an exportation of high-tech greed to sustain vapid and painful lives. What happens depends on how you pick the spirits, all of which are in contest for our future.

Your job would be much easier if you could turn to religions for quick sound advice. But alas! Religions attract bad spirits better than anything. Nothing makes the point more forcefully than the resurgence of religious wars. The European religious wars of the seventeenth century came to an end finally with the invention of the modern secular nation state. According to the polity of the secular nation state, religions were to be considered people's private affairs and to be tolerated so long as they did not infringe on other people's rights, especially those rights regarding the private practice of religion. This wholly secular conception of government did indeed put an end to those religious wars. But secular nation states in their turn give rise to economic wars of the sort that have devastated our own century. Part of the search for a "new world order" is the attempt to invent a polity that balances global responsibilities for economic and ecological matters with appropriate forms of local autonomy.

Meanwhile the collapse of imperial force in Eastern Europe has allowed deep-seated religious tensions to burst into battle. These tensions had been obscured from view because the truly secular mind cannot comprehend religion or its importance to people. Several months ago the *New York Times* did a summary chart of what it called "ethnic conflicts" around the world, analyzing forty-two of them. "Ethnic conflict" is what the secular *Times* calls a religious war. There are no ethnic differences between Serbians, Bosnians, and Croats; rather they are Orthodox, Muslim, and Roman Catholic, respectively. There are no ethnic differences between Catholics and Protestants in Northern Ireland, or between Sunnis and Shi'ites in Iraq and Iran, or between Armenian Christians and Muslim Azerbaijanis. These are wars between religions each of which has identified itself as determining a political culture. Surely there must be something religiously corrupt in these wars. When Buddhists who seek detachment and meditative enlightenment and Hindus whose slogan is *Shanti! Shanti! Shanti!*—peace, peace, peace—murder and rape one another in Sri Lanka, there must be something religiously corrupt. How is ethnic cleansing compatible with any religion that claims that its God or Path deserves universal respect? The problem is not lack of faith. In the midst of religious wars more fervent faith is the last thing that is needed: bring on the jaded skeptics! Rather, the problem is bad theology, theology that confuses the spirits.

In our secular world, we tend to think that theology is a matter of private religious belief. Or at least theology is to be confined to religious institutions and to the academy. But to the contrary, theology as the understanding required to test the spirits is a desperately needed public discourse. If these were not vacuum times that suck in spirits of all sorts, if these were not times of new opportunities for swarms of goods and evils, then we could leave theology to the ecclesiastical and academic theologians. But ours are the times that try our souls and fix our futures by the judgments and discernments we make of the spirits contending for our favor.

Nowhere has the failure of public theology been more evident than in the recent tragedy of David Koresh and the Branch Davidians. Part of our secular culture tried to look at them in moral categories and saw him as an opportunist; another part used psychological categories and saw him as crazy. But on either interpretation their mass suicide was inexplicable: according to the moralists they should have taken a better deal, and according to the psychologists they should have negotiated under pressure. But in fact the Branch Davidians did not commit suicide at all. They were fundamentally religious people, which is more important for their behavior than their moral orientations or psychological state: they immolated themselves in a triumphant affirmation of life in the face of overwhelming persecution, as guided by a profoundly mistaken theology. Their theology was mortally mistaken, and the rest of us did not even know theology was the issue! How far we are from the public theology we need!

Where shall you find the theology you need to test the spirits? I have two clues and a final quiz.

The first clue harks back to the theme of creation and origins. Religion is the cultural enterprise that displays human life as being under obligation. "Being under obligation" is a heavy phrase to lay upon you at a time of celebration although its meaning is simple enough. To be a human being is to face alternatives that differ in value, and we have the obligation to do the better. We have obligations to care for one another, to raise children well, to provide for economic security, to observe justice, and to respect and defer to those things of nature, society, and art whose worth should be recognized. Different cultures define the boundaries of obligations differently, but not as differently as we sometimes believe. Being under obligation defines the human condition. Pure relativism denies the stark obligatoriness of the human situation. To forget or evade obligations is to fail at humanity as well as at the specific obligations. Religion is what shapes cultures so that people know, feel, and behave as under obligation. Religion has thus a fundamental culture-building function. Without that religious function, cultures are amoral, nonhuman. The first clue for finding your public theology is to examine and assess how and where the religions of our society shape our culture's habits to behave as obligated persons. If ours is a culture of pure relativism, all our religions have failed.

The second clue, harking back to Elijah, lies in the fact that religion also has the function of assessing how well any given society lives up to its culturally defined obligations. Religion thus has a prophetic role in addition to the culture-building role. The shameful wars of religion in our time nearly always come when religions remember their culture-building functions but forget the prophetic or critical functions. Religions then identify with the cultures they build and lose the critical distance necessary for the prophetic roles. Public theology needs to test the spirits by determining whether they reflect proper moral judgments within and about society.

David Koresh's theology was defective in at least two ways. With regard to the culture-building function of religion it believed mistakenly that you could build a religious culture by withdrawing apart from the whole of society. With regard to the prophetic judgment of his culture, his theology failed to show him the contradiction between the assertion of his own privileges and the authority of the God in whose name he founded his community, a mistake Jesus, the servant, never made.

Now as to the quiz, do the spirits that tempt you lead to "love, joy, peace, patience, kindness, generosity, faithfulness, gentleness, and self-control?" If you can answer yes, your spirits have passed Paul's test in Galatians (5:22) for good spirits proved by their fruits. The creative venture for your generation is to determine what love means for a nation; what joy is for our civilization; what the shape of peace is among factions of ancient animosity; how patience is found for the slow processes of justice; what constitutes kindness in helping the weak, poor, and oppressed; how government can be generous without patronizing; how people can be faithful to their traditions while responsive to changes; how gentleness orders might to combat wrong; and how nations, civilizations, societies, governments, armies, peoples, and factions as well as you yourselves individually can exercise self-control in the face of enormous insecurity and competition.

The study of God and ultimate things might not be to your special taste, but it is crucial for your generation's theological task. The practice of some religious path in order to gain spiritual depth might not appeal to you now, but it is necessary for the theological task of your generation. Without knowledge and depth I fear you will become intoxicated by the wrong spirits. So many of us are tipsy and only babble.

In the long run there are no more important questions for your generation than, Which is the true God? and What spirits are the divine ones? The importance of the questions is not for your personal piety, although that too is important in its way. The importance is for your generation's calling in public life. The new cultural beginnings we inevitably will be enacting, consciously or unwittingly, need to discern divine winds of creative origins and prophetic morality. The other spirits are more tempting but toxic. So may God's Spirit rush upon you like a mighty wind and dance with flaming tongues of light and power on your heads. God bless you all. Amen.

Shortly after the previous Baccalaureate sermon at Boston University, I was invited to give a similar bureaucratic performance at Lehigh University. Alas, a week had passed and the lectionary texts were different; this is a new, but related sermon, delivered in the university church at Lehigh University on May 29, 1993. Coincidentally, this was the thirtieth anniversary of my ordination as a deacon.

24. Making Do in a Time with No Balm

Read and reflect on Jeremiah 8:18–9:1, Luke 16:1-13, 1 Timothy 2:1-7.

Let me add my welcome to those you have already heard. That welcome extends to the students in the Division of Religious and Theological Studies as well as to those in the School of Theology, and to the new staff and faculty in both. I recognize that the song we just sang about being anointed to preach good news to the poor, release to the captives, recovery of sight to the blind, and freedom to the oppressed might be construed narrowly to have application only to those in programs concerned with ordination. But construed generously, and with consciousness of the symbolic meanings of poverty, bondage, blindness, and oppression that have been with Western culture since the beginning, that anointing means simply that we are blessed to be alive with the responsibilities that obligate every human being.

To be human at all is to be obliged to help our sisters and brothers who are poor, in bondage, blind, or oppressed. The daily newspapers follow the Holy Scriptures in detailing the difficulties encountered in these responsibilities. Jeremiah put it bluntly: When we look for a balm in Gilead, it is not there. The Jeremiah text just prior to the passage read says God is sending enemy cavalry, earthquakes, and snakes. The passage following our text says the people are traitors, adulterers, and liars, and that God will lay waste the pastures, kill off the animals, and make Jerusalem a heap of ruins. So we have a biblical perspective, as it were, on the earthquakes in Asia, the killing storms, the epidemics of disease, the deceits of leaders, and the blind violence of wars that levels cities and ruins crops, on our tolerance of poverty, our bondage to corrupt institutions, our

160

blindness to both faults and virtues, and to the social fault lines of oppression. There is no balm in Gilead, and still we are supposed to bring relief.

Now I should tell you that the lectionary for today assigns a passage from 1 Timothy that Professor Allen said we don't have time to read. That is just as well, because the author of the epistles to Timothy matured greatly through his epistolary career. The first letter, you remember, contains the embarrassing passages about women being silent and never having authority over men. The third letter to Timothy, however, is a gem of sensitive advice with application to religious education in particular. On the topic of ministry in a time with no balm, 3 Timothy 9:37-38 says, "Do not look on the middle distance but keep your eyes on God's glory and concentrate on daily assignments. To worry about eventual success and failure is vain because the future belongs to God and you might not like it." That is my own translation from the Neo-Koine. Although some have questioned the authenticity of the text, I believe it represents an authentic Christian insight. Think of it in connection with Jesus' parable from Luke.

This parable of the dishonest manager who cheats his way out of a tight spot is not what you would expect from a high-minded religious figure such as you imagined Jesus to be. Imagine, praising a dishonest trickster! Now you will have to think twice about Jesus. For Jesus, salvation is worth it no matter what you have to do to get it. Jesus is not high-minded, but holy-minded. In this regard, as in so many, he stands in direct contrast to your faithful deans who make no claim to holiness but have a very high-minded attitude toward things such as plagiarism and cheating on tests. You will not be commended at all for cheating, no matter how shrewd or clever.

The theme of the trickster is widespread across many religions. The trickster is someone who gets what he or she wants by deceptive means that are contrary to common morality and sometimes to the law. One of the chief religious purposes of the trickster is to upset the common assumption that the universe runs on a moral system of rewards and punishments. God demands justice, as Jeremiah noted, but does not reward the good and punish the evil in this life. When we look in the middle distance at the moral outcomes of the universe, we see chaos. We admire the trickster, the clever bandit, Jacob tricking Esau and Laban, Solomon tricking the women fighting over the baby, and even the violent trickery of Roadrunner. There is something valid about the overturning of the moral story of life, although not for a minute is it legitimate for us to relax a jot or tittle of the moral responsibilities laid particularly upon us. Luke records Jesus making that point of moral rigorism just a few lines after this parable.

Jesus had a deeper point to the parable, however, than the trickster element, namely the conditions under which we are to live the responsible life. Suppose we identify with the rich man. With whom do we have to work to bring relief to poverty, bondage, blindness, and oppression? Honest and efficient managers, skilled and dedicated workers? Hardly. We have people like ourselves. Maybe even worse. You remember the old sermon title, "How can I soar like an eagle when I'm flying with these turkeys?"

More likely Jesus meant us to identify with the manager in the parable, the one commended for cleverness. His sinful nature fits us; and if we are this far along in higher education, we are clever in at least some ways. But Jesus' assessment of the manager is difficult to comprehend. He concludes the parable with what looks like a statement of its moral: "And I tell you, make friends for yourselves by means of dishonest wealth so that when it is gone, they may welcome you into the eternal homes." Part of what this means is what I said before, that Jesus urges finding salvation however possible, like the shepherd leaving ninety-nine sheep to search for the lost one, or the woman sweeping her whole house to find the lost coin, or the boy returning home in shame after squandering his wealth, the three preceding parables in Luke's account.

In this world, as Jeremiah knew, there is no honest wealth. So we have to make do with tainted stuff, with institutions that oppress, with families that abuse, with friends who betray, with teachers who scorn, with our own memories that forget, with minds that aren't sharp, with bodies that ache, with energies that tire, and with souls that despair. This is life. This is our lives. It doesn't get any better. There is little justice in life, at best good luck. There is no level playing field. To wake up to life's real rudeness is like suddenly losing a good job in which your faults seemed of no consequence with the result that you now have to live by your wits. To take this life and live it is faith. No wonder Jesus says you have to be shrewd to find salvation!

Leave it to Rabbi Jesus to make a hard point harder. In the lines after the parable, interpreting it, he suddenly shifts from shrewd morality to the heart of faith itself. He starts out with quantity: If you are faithful in a little, you will grow to be faithful in much, and if dishonest in small ways, you will become dishonest in much. Faith and wickedness expand.

Then Jesus moves to the object of faith: If you cannot be faithful when pursuing dishonest wealth, false gods, the life of ambition and greed, then you do not deserve a chance to be faithful to true riches, the true God. Better to sin with passion than to have no passion because without passion you would miss salvation even if God were in your lap.

Jesus then shifts to the ownership of faith: "If you have not been faithful with what belongs to another, who will give you what is your own?" This is a matter of pride for some of us. We reject the religion of our fathers and mothers, of our community and social class, because we see its childishness and superficialities, its corruptions and its history of hurting people. But if we cannot be faithful in someone else's religion, how can we have faith when we discover religion in a form we would like to own ourselves? This is a hard saying, especially for many of us liberals who have a nonembarrassing religion but cannot seem to get excited about it.

Jesus does not stop there. He turns up the heat on the quality of faith: You cannot have faith in two masters, for you will love one and hate the other. Faith is a singularity, it either is one thing or it is nothing. Faith might have many names, but only one heart. Our faith needs to grow from small things to great, or sin will grow instead. Our faith needs a depth of passion so as to deserve God as its true object. Our faith needs to be strong so that we can own it ourselves. And our faith needs to be a purity of heart to will one thing, as Kierkegaard so tellingly put it. Faith is strange, strong, upsetting, and very much like love.

Now this is the human condition. Life is tough, things are broken, the enemy is coming, and we are inadequate. But the good news is that no matter how bad things are, we can have faith. The gospel is that faith is ours if we will only receive it. Jesus' way to faith is through discipleship; and if we give ourselves to Jesus, the right faith will come at the right time. I invite you to that discipleship. Jesus' community of faith is the Christian movement that has transformed itself into faithful lives in cultures unimaginable to Jesus. That movement is as broken as the rest of the world, but it has fiery faith in it. You might have a classical Christology with high metaphysics or a unitarian anti-Christology, but the historical fact is that Jesus introduced a fire of faith that has remained burning through the wastelands and catastrophes of history. Think of the saints, broken all, but burning wicks of faith. Look at the windows: witnesses to faith. Touch your neighbor's elbow: there's a faith you can catch.

When you despair, are frustrated, and are discouraged about the blind devastations of nature and the foul violence of the human heart, stick to the little you can do and keep your eyes on Glory. Forget the middle distance of success and failure and give yourselves to God in faith that can grow you, focus you, take you over, and purify you. Faith feeds on Glory, and its work makes little broken things holy.

Now as to whether there is balm in Gilead, Jeremiah might not have the last word, for we have been sent the faith. Do you remember the song?

> Sometimes I feel discouraged, and think my work's in vain.
> But then the Holy Spirit revives my soul again.
> There is a balm in Gilead to make the wounded whole;
> There is a balm in Gilead to heal the sin-sick soul.

Welcome, Anointed! Amen.

This is another matriculation sermon for the School of Theology, preached in Marsh Chapel on September 21, 1995.

25. And There Was No King in Israel

Read and reflect on Judges 1:1-2, 17:6, 18:1, 19:1, 21.

From Exodus through Deuteronomy the Lord God had fought for Israel. Then the divine martial inertia, routinized in the charisma of Joshua, carried through the conquest of much of Canaan and gave the Israelites at least tentative settlement in their allotted lands. The book of Joshua concludes with the editorial comment that Israel faithfully served the Lord all the days of Joshua's generation who had witnessed God's mighty work.

But the book of Judges opens with a question supposing that the Lord God is no longer the warrior. Except for a felicitous flash flood that overturns Sisera's nine hundred iron chariots, and a strong divine encouragement to the Israelites to try for a third time to wipe out the warriors of Benjamin, which they do, going on to kill all the Benjaminite women and children and leaving only six hundred defeated soldiers huddling on a rock, the Lord God seems to have retired from battle in the time of the judges. Such success as the Israelites have in battle comes mainly from their own hand, and their successes are limited and ambiguous.

A nearly benign interpretation of this in looking to history as reported in the Bible to read God's character is that after the conquest of Canaan the Lord God comes to manifest more the character of the judge, dispensing justice, and less the character of a warrior. This accords with our own New Testament sensibilities. It also accords with the definition of kingship as messiah worked out in 1 Samuel, according to which a king is both warrior and judge.

So what about the Lord God's justice in the book of Judges? He does hold Israel to account for keeping the covenant. The editors who put

165

together the stories in Judges attempt to explain Israel's misfortunes by saying that the people periodically take the covenant lightly and worship the gods of other Canaanite peoples. But then the editors also say that the reason there are so many Canaanite peoples left, with such vigorous alternative gods and seductive sons and daughters, is that the Lord God wants the Israelites to be under constant temptation and military threat. If the Israelites tend to forget what God did for the preceding Exodus generation, then a little contemporary war is good for them, the argument goes. But now the Lord God is not fighting for them, and they have to struggle along themselves.

God's justice is hard to locate in the wars of the judges. When the Israelites are successful in battle, they tend either to kill off the enemy, man, woman, and child, or subject them to forced labor, as their own ancestors had been enslaved in Egypt, all with the Lord's blessing. To make matters worse, whereas the Egyptians had taken in the starving Israelites as welfare cases during famine and forced them to labor only when the Israelites' success threatened the Egyptian economy, the Israelites had come back into Canaan directly to exterminate or drive out the people of the land. If God be concentrating on justice rather than warfare in the time of the judges, why doesn't he encourage the Israelites to honor the native peoples of Canaan at least as resident aliens according to Moses' covenant law? Why doesn't he express disapproval of Ehud's treacherous murder of King Eglon (Judges 3:12-30) under a banner of peace? Why doesn't he tell Samson (Judges 14–16) to think with his head rather than other organs? Why doesn't the Lord God rage at the gang rape (Judges 19–21) of the Levite's concubine? Only the Israelites are upset. Contrast this divine silence to the closely parallel Genesis (19:1-21) story of gang rape in Sodom and Gomorrah, where the Lord God's response was to rain down fire and brimstone. When the Levite finds his concubine sprawled on the doorstep and says "Get up. We are going" (Judges 19:28), why doesn't the Lord God speak a word for sensitivity? Why does the Lord God encourage the Israelites to battle for a third time against Benjamin, and give them victory, without realizing that this would obliterate one of the twelve tribes? Can't God think ahead? It is not God but the Israelites who have qualms: "The people had compassion on Benjamin because the LORD had made a breach in the tribes of Israel" (Judges 21:15). And when people do realize what they have done, their "compassion" is to slaughter everyone in the town of Jabesh—man, woman, and child—except the four hundred virgin girls whom they give to the remaining six hundred Benjaminite soldiers. Justice? To satisfy the last two hundred Benjaminite soldiers they set up a general rape of young women celebrating the annual festival of the Lord in Shiloh in order that the girls' fathers might keep their legal oath not to give their daughters voluntarily to the men of Benjamin, all with God's silent approval. I think Mary Daly read the book of Judges. It is difficult to tell who is the most unjust, crude, and thoughtless character in that book, but surely the Lord God, as depicted in those stories, is a leading candidate.

My own favorite character is Shamgar, the judge who killed six hundred Philistines with an oxgoad (Judges 3:31). To be able to do so much with so little, he would have made a good dean. The scholar Robert Boling points out that Shamgar was most likely a mercenary working for the cult of the warrior/goddess Anath, with no affiliation whatsoever with the Lord God of Israel. That he slew the Philistines for reasons of his own had the side-effect of rescuing Israel, who thus remembered him as a judge. At least Shamgar was effective and played no deliberate or intentional role in the bloody story of Israel and its Lord God. The conclusion of Judges is that there is no King in Israel, and all the people did what was right in their own eyes. Indeed, there is no king in Israel, on the ground or in heaven, at the end of Judges.

I will leave Professor Parker to explain what the Deuteronomist editors meant by arranging the stories to open with the need for the people to take over God's previous military work and to close with moral chaos of people and divinity. I want to ask more directly what we can learn from all this. Let me suggest two points.

One is that Judges is the first realistic book in the order of the Bible with regard to human affairs and God's management. No good social arrangement lasts for long, as Joshua's grandchildren learned. If your enemies don't get you first, you will ruin your own affairs. There is no enduring good side, but every side is selfish, treacherous, and ready to justify itself by reference both to past victimization and to the blessings of God. The judges' divinely commanded ethnic cleansing on all sides reminds us of Bosnia and Rwanda.

The realism of Judges destroys conclusively the anthropomorphic myth that God arranges human affairs to reward justice, punish evil, and cultivate Israel as a nation of holy priests. That anthropomorphic view of providence is still popular today with people who over-personalize God or who want God to be a king on our side rather than God of all. This dangerous symbolism is expressed frequently in the Torah, although qualified there by a shattering

167

divine holiness that breaks the personal model. The Deuteronomist editors try to carry it on in the later historical writings, as when the Lord God promises to keep a descendant of David on the throne of Israel forever.

But Israel lost its kingdom, as we know. If the Jews are chosen beneficiaries of divine promotion, their history is a very strange way of revealing that. The Nazi holocaust was a devastating refutation that God takes care of Israel in that anthropomorphic way, punishing only the evil and rewarding those who keep the covenant. But the moral at the end of Judges is even more stark: The people of Israel commit near genocide on themselves, saving a smaller proportion of Benjamin than escaped the Nazi ovens, a bloody, wicked salvation effected by the people to correct God's mistake. By the end of Judges, the Israelites have lost their former putative hegemony over Canaan and have sunk into moral chaos whose symbol is their God.

Hear carefully what I am saying. My point is not that God in fact is evil or impetuous and confused. It is that, *if* you think of God as an agent hovering over and in history making things work out for the best, rewarding the good and punishing the evil, then a realistic look at history will wake you from that dreaming innocence. Real history reveals the symbol of God, so conceived, to be evil, impetuous, and incompetent. The book of Judges is a powerful corrective to childish theology, however attractive that simple personalism is even to us.

The second point to learn from Judges is even more devastating to our desire to have a simple and anthropomorphic vision of God. We sometimes would like to think that we can learn about the real God from stories. Some theologians today such as Stanley Hauerwas believe that the way to understand Christianity in the modern world is by telling stories of how we are "resident aliens." Some feminist theologians believe that women will find their true identity before God and one another by telling their stories. There was a theological fashion in my youth to interpret Christianity according to a large story called "salvation history." Oscar Cullmann was the biblical theologian associated with that movement, but the story has had many forms other than his.

No sequence of events is only one story. There is a different story for every actor in the sequence. Consider the plot of Joshua and Judges from the standpoint of the Amorites, Perizzites, Hivites, Hittites, and Jebusites. Or the Philistines, whom in others of our own Western myths of origin we revere as the daring and smart Phoenicians who gave us our alphabet. Or consider the events just from the side of the Israelites, where one telling of the story makes sense of obedience and disobedience to the Lord God and another shows that obedience to be bloody and wholly unjust according to the morals of the Torah. The book of Judges, perhaps despite itself, makes manifestly clear that one should be very careful drawing any moral from a story, either about God or about virtue and justice.

Nowhere is this better expressed than in the Song of Deborah in Judges 5, one of the oldest texts of the entire Bible. The Israelites then were marauders living in the hills who plundered the caravans of the more civilized city states of Canaan. The Canaanites hired a Philistine mercenary, Sisera, with nine hundred iron chariots, to protect their roads and plains. Deborah, the Israelite judge and war chieftain, and Barak, her somewhat wimpy partner, defeated Sisera when the Lord God caused a flash flood that overturned the chariots. Jael, a non-Israelite woman, offered to hide and protect Sisera, but instead drugged and murdered him by driving a tent-peg through his head. The next to last scene in the Song of Deborah, the most poignant in the entire book of Judges, is of Sisera's mother wondering aloud to her handmaidens why he is so late coming home from the day's battle, expressing concern and taking dubious comfort in the thought he is collecting the spoils. We know he has been betrayed and murdered, and her questions tug at our hearts with her mother's love. The last scene shifts back to Deborah who says, "So perish all your enemies, O LORD! But may your friends be like the sun as it rises in its might." From whose story do we draw a moral here? The Lord God's? Israel's? The Canaanite city states? Deborah's? Jael's? Sisera's? His mother's? Deborah's bloodthirsty closing surely cannot be the moral if mercy is a divine trait and human virtue.

That we fool ourselves in trying to learn from stories does not mean that we should not learn from history, however. The difference is that history ideally includes all the stories from all perspectives, and many factors that do not fit into story form at all. What history shows in the instance of Judges is that God has to be God of all the people. The partisan God of the Israelites is a wicked and incompetent *agent provocateur*. The true Lord of history suffers with Sisera's mother, with the Levite's concubine as well as the Levite, with Benjamin's rapists as well as the vengeance-seekers from the rest of Israel, with fat, trusting Eglon as well as sly Ehud. That God transcends story to encompass all perspectives does not suggest that the morality of anyone is not obligatory or that evil is merely relative. But it does say that stories are ambiguous and that God cannot be conceived as a person with a singular perspective on one side's story.

What and who God is cannot be conceived easily. The historical realism of Judges pushes our imaginations back to the scary Holy One of Israel and even farther back to the Creator of all things, including persons and the ambiguous stories of history. It pushes our thoughts forward to the God of love whose love is not personal except in us but is redemptive of history's ambiguities and alienations. Judge's realism deconstructs our partisan domestic gods. It causes us to ask for God in Israel but also in Canaan, in human history but also beyond. It leads us to look for love but not favor and for glory but not success. It pushes us to praise the God who is higher than our ambitions and deeper than our stories. There may be no king in Israel, but praise the Almighty and Glorious king of the cosmos, revealed to us in our moral chaos.

The book of Judges does not contain a group of consistently edifying stories. Maybe Gideon wasn't so bad, but most of the characters, Israelite or anti-Israelite, were bloodthirsty for Yahweh at best but more often parochial, petty, weak, adolescent (think of Samson and his gonads), or vicious. But worst of all was God! Professor Simon Parker, who taught the Hebrew Bible class in 1995 assigned me Judges to preach on in Robinson Chapel on October 4.

26. PERPLEXITIES OF HISTORY

Read and reflect on Isaiah 39.

P oor Isaiah could not make sense of history any better than I. He began
with the conviction, common from his day to ours, that history's sense
lies in the struggle between good and evil and that God rewards the good
while punishing the evil. This was a plain moral to be drawn from the stories of Adam and Eve, Cain and Abel, Noah, and a host of others. In addition, Isaiah assumed a special relation of God to Abraham's descendants
in which, if the people were faithful, God would make them flourish as a
folk possessing a land flowing with milk and honey. The great covenants
with Abraham and Moses make this point. Even further, Isaiah assumed a
special relation of God to Jerusalem and the House of David such that the
dynasty would be preserved even if some of the kings did not measure up
to David's stature. This was the direct sense of the covenant between
Yahweh and David reported in 2 Samuel 7. These three elements—the
moral character of the universe, the destiny of his people, and the everlasting political authority of the House of David—would seem to provide
a clear framework for the interpretation of history. Yet history gave the lie
to all three.

From our perspective we see that the histories of Israel and Judah were
determined mainly by the brute geopolitical forces of the time. The forty
years or so of Isaiah's flourishing in the last half of the eighth century was
the time of the arising of the Assyrian empire in competition with Egypt,
and both Israel and Judah were caught up in that power play. Desperate
and sometimes foolish attempts to ally themselves with the Egyptians,
Syrians, or other peoples may have bought a little time, more time for

Judah than for Israel; but the Assyrians were coming, and after them the Babylonians, the Persians, the Greeks, the Romans, the Arabs, the Normans, the Arabs again, and the British.

Isaiah tried desperately to preserve the ideology of the moral order, giving virtue credit for victories and blaming defeats and suffering on moral and cultic vice. But the problem, doubtless evident to Isaiah himself, was that there are *always* some virtuous people and *always* some vicious ones, and the dynamic of history is driven rather by the advancing power of the Assyrians as barely qualified by various distractions. Part of the structure of First Isaiah is its contrasting of bad King Ahaz with good King Hezekiah, but in both cases they just squeak by, supported by accidents attributed to God. Isaiah can cite this as evidence of Yahweh's loyalty to the House of David, bad or good; but the House of David was diminishing on the world scene in the original Isaiah's time and later, in fact, finally fell. Our thirty-nine chapters of First Isaiah contain many interpolations from the later witnesses to the exile of the House. The book ends with double irony as Hezekiah flirts with the Babylonian enemies of the Assyrians who in fact will bring down Assyria, but also Jerusalem and the House of David. Isaiah's questions in this incident indicate well-founded suspicion. When he tells Hezekiah that his goods and family will be carried off to Babylon and his sons made eunuchs, Hezekiah, amazingly, approves the prophecy because it means his own time will have peace. This is the good king? We cannot but think of Neville Chamberlain's statement after the Munich Pact with Hitler that "We will have peace in our time," whereupon Hitler moved into the Sudetenland and Poland. Surely the editors arranged our text to end with this story to make the point that history is truly ambiguous.

Isaiah and his later editors tried hard to make sense of history according to the old codes. There is a regular and steady insistence on the importance of righteousness and the faithfulness of God's justice. Applied to events, however, this perspective leads to a bewildering jumble of praises, anathemas, and empty promises of restoration. Read rapidly through the thirty-nine chapters of First Isaiah, and the impression is of desperate judgmental overkill. The Daughter of Zion is destined to draw all nations to herself; yet she is desolated, likened to Sodom and Gomorrah, and will suffer even worse later. The surrounding nations too, including Assyria, seem at once to flourish as the instruments of Yahweh and to stand in ruins or to be destined for desolation. Isaiah desperately tries to line up virtue and flourishing, vice and destruction. But the overall effect is confusion and a straining at the evidence that undermines the principles.

Isaiah wrote over a period about as long as the time from the end of the Second World War until now. At the end of the war Americans were rather confident that virtue had triumphed and that God had settled peace on the throne in the form of the United Nations, strategically located in New York. How foolish that seems now! Nothing of 1950 seems now as it did then, whether in world politics, economics, or the state of the environment. When President Clinton campaigned for office by saying that the Vietnam War was morally ambiguous, he told a truth whose reference is far wider. Everything in history is morally ambiguous, a mixture of triumph and suffering, good for some but dreadful for others, fulfilling promises but leading to destruction. This is not to say that there are no clear moral obligations or that justice cannot be defined and pursued. It is only to say that nothing is ever only one thing. There is no one story. Every incident participates in many stories.

And there is something worse about history: It proceeds according to the forces of causation, not according to moral deserts. Wars are won by the bigger armies with the better generals. Prosperity comes from industry and the luck of the market, and conniving helps. Suffering is caused by germs, by drought, and by the sudden appearance of the barbarians. Yahweh said, in Exodus 3, "I have come down to deliver them from the Egyptians, and to bring them up out of that land to a good and broad land, a land flowing with milk and honey, to the country of the Canaanites, the Hittites, the Amorites, the Perizzites, the Hivites, and the Jebusites." Imagine the historical perplexity of the Canaanite's version of Isaiah when the warlord Joshua led the Hebrew barbarians across the river to establish strongholds in the hills whence to raid the fertile valleys. What sins of the Canaanites, Hittites, Amorites, Perizzites, Hivites, or Jebusites called their gods to punish them? None that Yahweh explained to Moses. They simply were in the way of the Hebrew migration. Second Isaiah would have understood this point, and probably First Isaiah sensed it too—brute forces of history compounded by the accidental crossing of two peoples' stories. The droughts, floods, earthquakes, and plagues are accidents, each caused by understandable physical forces but impinging by chance on the stories of individuals and nations.

First Isaiah is witness to the confusion history throws at Providence when Providence is supposed to be governed by moral deserts rather than causal forces, by preferential treatment of a people, or by the divine protection of a ruling house. We now see the wisdom of the later editors who inserted the apocalyptic material of chapters 24–27. When the human hermeneutic fails, go back to the foundations of creation. The Holy Terror Yahweh does not dally with the world but can undo the first days of creation, break up the earth, mix the saltwater and fresh, turn out the lights: "For the windows of heaven are opened, and the foundations of the earth tremble. The earth is utterly broken, the earth is torn asunder, the earth is violently shaken" (Isaiah 24:18-19). So much for the biased champion of Israel and the House of David. God is in charge, but Providence is not what we might think.

Now apocalyptic writing is very strange indeed, and Professor Darr will explain it to you in full detail later. Let me here call attention to only one of its characteristics and draw two consequences that help us see how the gospel stands with regard to the perplexities of history as well as of our personal lives. Apocalyptic writing testifies to the infinity of God's holiness with maximal intensity and exaggeration. It takes the stuff of history—people, places, events, time, and the future—and so charges them with God's holiness that they are transformed from their usual meaning. In the nonapocalyptic parts of First Isaiah judgment and retribution are directed against specific peoples, cities, and kings; in the Isaiah Apocalypse, everything will be destroyed, all people, all cities, even the heavens and the earth. Apocalyptic promises both destruction and redemption for the future, but not a real historical future. Fundamentalists have tried to rehistoricize apocalyptic to predict end times. But this misses the point that history itself is transformed in apocalyptic: judgment and promise are for God's time, not ours. In apocalyptic, history becomes a mere metaphor for the Holy Reality of God; indeed, apocalyptic changes the topic from creation to creator, and all creation becomes a metaphor for an infinite terrifying Holy Love that can no more fit neatly into history than Yahweh could fit into Mount Sinai without burning and breaking out on all around.

The first consequence of apocalyptic is that the demand for justice and righteousness is not metaphorized but intensified. From chapter 1 through 39 First Isaiah insists on God's demand for justice and the moral penalty for evil. Therefore the later editors were not subverting things to insert the apocalyptic vision of the destruction of the evil world, punishment for atonement, and restitution of Israel as a new vineyard, one without the grapes of wrath. The editors only intensified the demand for justice to an ultimate degree: the very creation of the world demands justice, even when within history the just suffer and the evil flourish. From this we may conclude with First Isaiah that we must seek justice regardless. Even when there are no rewards except to the wicked, we must persevere in righ-

174

teousness. Even when our justice is partial and the institutions of suffering and oppression seem intractable, we must pursue righteousness as far as we can. Even when projects are cut off, when accidents blight good intentions, when life fragments into the meaningless disruptions of history's blind forces, we must be faithful to justice in great things and small. When in the brute history of cosmic expanding gases the earth is reduced to ruins and no niche is possible for carbon bodies such as we, we will be judged by our pursuit of justice in our short time.

The second consequence of apocalyptic is its revelation that we live in the infinite God as well as in finite history. The meaning of our lives is in how we keep the faith in the finite, fragmented, and blind forces of history; this is the life we have and no other. The heresy of Gnosticism misses this point. But on the other hand, the true place of our identity, our true home, is in the infinite life of the Holy God who creates us. The finiteness of our lives is infinite in God. Where we are fragmented, broken, and unfinished, God's life is infinitely whole. Where history is morally meaningless except for the question of how we have kept the faith, history is most truly the creature of God, existing by infinite love, blessed in its very existence. Apocalyptic expresses this in metaphors of divine banquets, lush vineyards, damnation of evil, and the joys of angelic song. Yet the topic is not those things but God as completing the creation in divine glory.

Against the apocalyptic background of the infinite seriousness of justice and the extraordinary contrast between our finite lives and their infinite home in Glory, the power of the Christian gospel stands stark and terrifying in its way. For Jesus is the way to faithful justice in a finite world, justice misunderstood, unappreciated, frustrated, cut short, partial, and rewarded with the cross. We who pick up Jesus' life alike must engage our tasks, expecting the same limitations, fragmentations, and premature endings, confident with Isaiah that somehow the way of justice is the only way for us. Jesus is also the way home to God, to the Creator, to the Love itself that glories in our lives. We who follow Jesus follow through the fire and smoke of Sinai, across the Deep River Jordan, across the abyss that separates the infinite from the finite to the infinite light that is our glory and God's. The miracle of Jesus the Christ is that, unlike the shaky divine temporary inhabitation of Mount Sinai, the infinite Holy God dwells fully and neatly in Jesus. Jesus joins the resurrection to the cross's reconciliation of justice with history's blindness. Jesus is the Way to be a finite creature of an infinite Holy and Loving Creator. Jesus' Way meets us in our weakness, fear, and sin to take us to God. Jesus' identity comes as much from infinite

Holiness as from the finite starts and stops of history. Jesus is the infinite light itself coming into our darkness. When we enter into that light, we see our way through this blind darkness and know that this is the way home. In us Jesus is God creating us and loving us into Glory. With Isaiah we commit ourselves to justice and bow to judgment even when justice is partial, unrewarded, and ambiguous. With Isaiah we trust the Lord who gives life and takes it away, who sends both rain and drought, succor and barbarians, who raises up the Houses of David and Assyria and brings them down, whose world runs blindly, whose history is brute force, and whose holiness brings blessing and glory in it all. From Isaiah to Jesus to the saints of our place we see the Holy One of Israel calling us to love through justice in our time into God's immense eternity. Thanks be to God whose holiness rolls on mercy. Amen.

This is the sermon for the Hebrew Bible Class for November 3, 1993. Professor Darr assigned Isaiah.

Part Five
Christian Intelligence

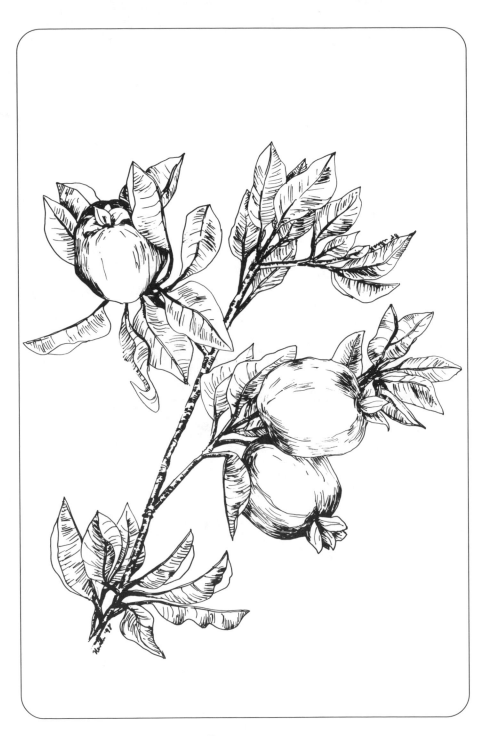

Pomegranate

27. CHRISTIAN INTELLIGENCE
AND WORLDLY FOOLISHNESS

Read and reflect on Micah 6:1-8, 1 Corinthians 1:18-31,
Matthew 5:1-12.

Ordinarily I am deeply appreciative of the writings of Paul. Nearly everyone here, except perhaps the new students, knows that I devote what little research creativity I have to the study of Paul's third letter to Timothy. That letter is particularly interesting to me because Timothy was, I believe, at the time the letter was addressed to him, the dean of Troas University School of Theology. Unraveling the historical context of that letter holds many lessons for us today. For instance, we can understand much of the tragic beginnings of patriarchal authoritarianism in the Christian church from the overreactions of Timothy at TUSTH to the attacks on him from the sister institution at Ephesus. As we know from Luke's account in Acts 19, Ephesus had been a hotbed of what we now would call radical feminism long before the Christian movement there. The ancient tradition had worshiped the goddess Artemis, and it appears from indirect evidence that the Christian seminary there, the Ephesians Divinity School, had represented Jesus as the consort of Artemis, dying each year and rising again after the pattern of Osiris. A document brought to my attention by Professor Darr contains an immoderate radical feminist attack on Timothy's integrity by a person named Debra, whom I have discovered to be the same person as the valedictorian of the first class to graduate from EDS; one Debra, Daughter of Demetrius. Perhaps Professors Smith and Sampley can review the Ephesian evidence in their New Testament classes in order to bring more of you into this fascinating, if tragic, episode in Christian history. This fascination is but a small part of my devotion to the writings of Paul and I encourage you not to limit your study of his writings to 3 Timothy.

But Paul is not always helpful. His text for today from 1 Corinthians, contrasting worldly wisdom that God makes foolishness with the foolishness of the cross that God makes saving wisdom, is paradoxically dangerous because it is so liable to misinterpretation. A great many people respond to that text as a license for anti-intellectualism. They identify literature, science, history, politics, indeed all erudition whatsoever, with the "wisdom of the world," and dismiss it as having been overturned by God. And instead they seize upon such simple formulas as "Jesus Christ Crucified" as sufficient to guide their lives and that of the church. This is a disastrous situation that threatens the very life of the church today. Paul's admonition in 3 Timothy 19:4—"Don't let ignorance masquerade as virtue"—is as true and important today as in Timothy's time.

Let me hasten to say what I do *not* mean when I attack anti-intellectualism. I do not mean that all Christians have to be learned. On the contrary, Jesus gave special attention to the poor and victimized; and Christianity is a religion for all people, of all classes, of all accomplishments or lack thereof, and of all talents. Neither learning nor ignorance has the slightest merit for salvation itself. Nor do I mean to deny that poor people have an intelligence and wisdom of their own. Street smarts is often far more to the point than academic learning. Nor do I mean that intellectual accomplishment is positively associated with spiritual accomplishment; simple, uneducated people often have a far more profound spirituality than sophisticates who know too much in the head to know anything in the heart. Nor do I mean that all leadership in religion needs to be intellectually sophisticated. Many denominations in the so-called "free-church" tradition ordain ministers without benefit of seminary education, or even college or high school education; often these ministers are successful in their congregations.

What I mean is that Christian intelligence is one office of the church's ministry, and that the timely and well-placed exercise of this office is absolutely indispensable to the practice of the gospel of Christ. Without the cultivation of informed intelligence to the utmost, Christian ministry becomes stupidified, banal, and boring.

What is Christian intelligence? Reflect on the lectionary texts, beginning with that from Paul. "For Jews demand signs and Greeks desire wisdom, but we proclaim Christ crucified, a stumbling block to Jews and foolishness to Gentiles, but to those who are the called, both Jews and Greeks, Christ the power of God and the wisdom of God."

According to the wisdom of the Jewish world, the sign that Jesus was the Messiah would be that Israel were made an independent nation to which

Rome would pay tribute, and that did not happen. Christian intelligence must be able to articulate the new sense of Messiahship with new senses of messianic authority and of discipleship. Further, according to the wisdom of the Jewish world, to claim that Jesus is divine in any sense would be abhorrent idolatry. Christian intelligence must be able to articulate a new sense of God that integrates the person of Jesus and the presence of the Holy Spirit into the nature and work of the Creator.

According to the wisdom of the Greek world, crucifixion is a demeaning way to die and marks the victim as one of life's minor losers, not to be compared with noble Socrates or larger-than-life Alexander. Christian intelligence must be able to say how and in what sense God works with the mean and lowly and why failure, suffering, being misidentified and put to death at an early age as a common criminal is the true way to glory. As to resurrection, according to Greek wisdom returning from the dead is a fairly common mythic theme and rarely signifies glorious victory, usually only a chance to finish one's work, sometimes a second chance to do better. Christian intelligence must find a meaning to resurrection that signifies something worth going through crucifixion to attain.

So far we have found that Christian intelligence must discern for the practice of our time what it means for Jesus to be Messiah and Lord, if we are to know what to do and what to avoid as disciples of Christ. We have found that we need a Trinitarian theology, or some alternative, that explains for the terms in which we live today how Jesus is or how he is not to be regarded as divine. We have found that Christian intelligence must provide an interpretation of the human condition that finds glory in finitude, contrary to the expectation of this and nearly every other age. These are the topics of theology plain and simple.

Consider the text from Micah. The Lord who brought Israel out of Egypt and saved them again and again is offended that the people think their response should be elaborate sacrifice; rather what the Lord requires is "to do justice, and to love kindness, and to walk humbly with your God." Far more difficult than the observation of ritual sacrifice, the pursuit of justice requires knowing what hurts and what helps people, knowing how to cause an improvement rather than an impoverishment, knowing how to help people without enslaving them to charity, knowing how to honor other people's responsibility while helping them do well themselves. To do justice, love kindness, and walk humbly with God requires knowing what to do in Bosnia, Somalia, Ireland, and India. It requires learning how to increase wealth without increasing poverty. Holiness before God is not a pious sentiment but behavior that effectively carries God's redeeming grace to our neighborhoods and ourselves; where we do not understand how to do that, we do more harm than good and frustrate the divine purpose. So the practice of the Christian life requires informed intelligence.

Consider finally the Beatitudes as expressed in the text from Matthew. Jesus said there that we ought to prize the characters of poverty of spirit, mournfulness, meekness, deficiency of righteousness but a hunger for it, mercifulness, purity of heart, peacemaking habits, suffering for righteousness, and endurance of slander. Contrast that list with the definition of virtuous character in the Boy Scout Law: trustworthiness, loyalty, helpfulness, friendliness, courtesy, kindness, obedience, cheerfulness, thriftiness, bravery, cleanliness, and reverence. The Scout Law is what worldly wisdom defines as virtue after nineteen hundred years of Christian influence. Why do Jesus' beatitudes still seem so odd? It's not that the Boy Scouts are wrong about virtue, but that Jesus said there is something deeper and more important to value. Jesus has called us to see, appreciate, and feel the world in a new and strange way, a way more like God's, he thought. How do we understand this? What is this new vision of value to which Christians are called? More than theology in the broad sense, more than Christian ethics and holiness, Christian intelligence is needed to prize the world divinely. Perhaps that is the most revolutionary element of Christianity, its new taste, its novel discernment of spirits.

Christian intelligence is the ministerial office of theology, ethics, and taste that provides the means by which God's renewing grace is grasped and lived out in faith. Learned intelligence is required to interpret and appropriate the sources of our common ministry and life in the Bible and in our history; so we must thus cultivate the intelligence of erudite hermeneutics. Learned intelligence is required to grasp the world we live in, to see how the gospel both judges and brings renewal to the world in its many different conditions; so we must cultivate the intelligence of the sciences, the practical disciplines of politics and economics, and of the arts of creation and imagination. Failure to understand and press through to a radical questioning of the sources of grace within the tradition and the conditions of our contemporary situations is to deny that the gospel makes any difference beyond the do-goodism of current fashion.

Christianity is growing explosively in parts of the world and among conditions of people where the office of Christian intelligence seems largely unnecessary and unnoticed. Across the Third World and in some sections of North America there are people whose lives are so hopeless and whose native religion is so corrupt or vacant that the simple gospel story of Jesus, without intellectual embellishment or background, provokes the spirit of renewal. After all, the gospel is simply that God loves you and the others as well. It would be entirely inappropriate to insist that ministry in those situations needs much of the office of Christian intelligence as I have been defining learned ministry. Even the seminaries in many parts of the world have nonintellectual demands that are far more important than intellectual ones. But when by the power of the gospel people do regain hope, they shall come to ask what to hope for, and they shall need the gospel's theology in rigorous form adequate to the day. When by the power of the gospel people have seized onto life, they shall come to ask how to live in a complex world where they make a difference for better or worse; and they shall need to know the gospel's implications for justice and holiness. When by the power of the gospel people wake up to the fact they are loved by God and buoyed through life's constant crucifixions by infinite grace, they shall come to ask what really is worthwhile and what really is at stake in their new life within God; and they shall require learned discernment and taste in valuing things through the divine vision. Someplace, if not in Peru or Roxbury, the passion for Christian intelligence must be pursued relentlessly for the sake of the faith's mission.

In North America, the mainline denominations, which have had traditions of learned ministry, are now suffering the losses that derive from boredom, triviality, and stupidity. The remedy has been vainly sought in increased social services and in attempts to think and speak like the culture in its various forms. But people rightly see that we do not need religion for an improved politics or for cultural solidarity and indulgence. The gospel is new news every day; and if it is not presented with its transformative power, the social costs of institutionalized religion are too high to pay. The remedy for the North American mainline churches can only be a new articulation of the gospel that answers the challenges of modernity, that responds to the issues of secularism, and that enables us to sort the grace from the dross in our history and institutions. Without learned ministry, without pushing Christian intelligence to its most strenuous, we shall either repeat the tradition irrelevantly or mirror our culture's narcissism. The wisdom of the cross is indeed not worldly wisdom, and it looks foolish from the worldly perspective. But it is wisdom nevertheless, which requires a constant struggle of understanding and application. Although Jesus wept over Jerusalem, anticipated his crucifixion with dread, and unleashed his temper on the money changers, his deepest expressions of frustration and anger were reserved for his disciples when they did not understand. Learned ministry is an ancient challenge. Welcome to its responsibilities. You shall be needed. Amen.

This was the matriculation sermon for spring 1993, preached on January 28 in Marsh Chapel. It makes more than usual full use of 3 Timothy. The commonly used acronym for the Boston University School of Theology is BUSTH. We have some friendly rivalry with the Episcopal Divinity School (EDS) in Cambridge, known for its very strong feminism.

28. HOW TO BE RICH
AFTER PAYING TUITION

Read and reflect on Joel 2:23-30, 1 Timothy 6:6-19, Luke 16:19-31.

Permit me to add my welcome to the voices you have already heard. Let me in fact welcome back the faculty, staff, and continuing students as well as new students, because in many ways we all begin each year anew and need to recollect ourselves for our work together.

The three texts read today are this week's lectionary readings, and they all deal with riches. They don't say the same thing about riches, however. Joel promises riches as a divine reward. Jesus' parable in Luke, by contrast, seems to say that being rich by itself sends one to Hades, while being poor sends one to Heaven; I'll suggest a different interpretation. Paul's advice to Timothy warns not about wealth but about obsessive concern about wealth: "the *love* of money is the root of all evil." You can tell from my sermon title that I am not against wealth, that I have a plan for how you should spend yours, namely on tuition, and that I am confident that you can be rich afterward.

Let us consider first the passage from 1 Timothy. It immediately follows Paul's warning against those who believe that godliness is a means toward worldly gain. That warning applies to many in our society who assume that belonging to the right church is as good as belonging to the right country club. Paul recommends, by contrast, that the pursuit of godliness ought to be combined with contentment, and that contentment means being satisfied with our condition so long as we have food and clothing. Rich and poor alike should remember Paul's line, "You can't take it with you."

In the Second Letter to Timothy, at 3:1-5, Paul radicalized the point about money and gave it an eschatological context, writing:

185

You must understand this, that in the last days distressing times will come. For people will be lovers of themselves, lovers of money, boasters, arrogant, abusive, disobedient to their parents, ungrateful, unholy, inhuman, implacable, slanderers, profligates, brutes, haters of good, treacherous, reckless, swollen with conceit, lovers of pleasure rather than lovers of God, holding to the outward form of godliness but denying its power. Avoid them!

But it was in his Third Letter to Timothy that Paul directly addressed our theme. By way of context I should acknowledge that scholars have known for a long time that the pastoral epistles, including those to Timothy, were not written by the apostle Paul himself but by someone later who represented Paul's school. The first two letters to Timothy have the form of advice given by an older father-figure to a young man in the early stages of his career. The third letter, however, most likely dates from twenty years later, and I believe it can be shown that Timothy at that time was the dean of the theological school at Troas, an institution most likely founded involuntarily by Paul. Second Timothy 4:13 says, "When you come, bring the cloak that I left with Carpus at Troas, also the books, and above all the parchments." There is no record of the books and parchments ever being returned, and they appear to be the beginnings of the Troas University School of Theology library. Incidentally, we know from history that Troas was decisive for East-West developments in Christianity, and in this respect founded the tradition of theological education that has flourished for so many years at the Boston University School of Theology. The style of 3 Timothy is not that of a father-figure writing to a son but rather that of a worried alumnus writing to a dean. I receive many letters of this genre. In this context, then, we may understand the following text from 3 Timothy 4:6-8:

Students should not complain about tuition or the high cost of living but should be grateful to the saints who make their education possible, remembering finite generations in gifts to the alumnae/i fund. Whether rich or poor, students should combine contentment in what the Lord provides with the expectation that their ministry will lead them into trials that cannot be anticipated and for which no preparation can be wholly satisfactory. For, although we cannot take worldly riches with us, we are richly borne into eternity by the infinite grace of God which provides when money is short, renews when we are exhausted, inspires when learning falls short, comforts when we fail, and arms us to fight the good fight when we are broken, lost, betrayed, overwhelmed, and defeated by the world's standards.

Notice that there are three important variables in Paul's remarks: paying tuition as a part of commitment to ministry, trust in God's rich grace, and a depiction of ministry as a struggle that we are likely to lose according to the world's standards.

Think for a moment about Paul's image of ministry. All the letters to Timothy are filled with grim images of betrayal, suffering, imprisonment, and the collapse of churches that Paul had founded and that had once seemed so promising. Writing after Paul's death, the Pauline author of the letters knew that Paul's life did not, in fact, have a happy ending by worldly standards. I pray that those of you who go into ordained ministry, or into Christian ministry in a broader sense, or into careers of ministry to scholarship and teaching will have successful lives filled with love and friendship and crowned by a comfortable retirement package. But there is no Christian promise of that. Rather, the Christian images warn of the opposite, the primary image being crucifixion.

Paul's second variable was the stress on God's grace as true wealth beyond worldly riches. This theme is constant throughout the authentic letters of Paul as well as the pastoral letters. In our lectionary text from 1 Timothy Paul wrote: "As for those who in the present age are rich. . . . They are to do good, to be rich in good works, generous, and ready to share, thus storing up for themselves the treasure of a good foundation for the future, so that they may take hold of the life that really is life." The "life that really is life" is the gift of God's infinite grace.

With this in mind we may allegorize the lesson from Joel, which was originally intended to have a political and economic reference. The life of Christians, from a worldly standpoint, might well look as if it had been razed by the swarming locust, the hopper, the destroyer, the cutter, and the great army God sends to plague us. But we should be glad, for in Christ God has sent us the early rain that brings great harvest so that we shall eat and be satisfied; and for our spirits God will pour out the Holy Spirit on our flesh, our sons and daughters shall prophesy, our old people shall dream dreams, the young shall see visions, and even the oppressed and enslaved shall be bathed by the Spirit's balm. The real meaning of the crucifixion is its connection with the resurrection, not what the world sees.

As to Paul's point about tuition, it should be remembered that there were very few endowed scholarships at Troas University, nor was there much financial assistance at TUSTH. Paying tuition was emblematic of the much larger Christian project of steady commitment in the face of adversity, uncertainty, and bad news. Paul's remark was the educational parallel to his martial remark about fighting the good fight and the athletic remark about running the race set before us. Paying tuition is part of the hard work of sustaining a steady intentionality about carrying through the vision of the Christian life. There are many difficult parts of life that must be shaped and organized around the overall project of living so as to cast ourselves upon the riches God provides. When we lose sight of that higher vision, the pursuit of wealth becomes an obsession that leads us into all manners of temptations so that, as Paul said in 1 Timothy, we are "trapped by many senseless and harmful desires that plunge people into ruin and destruction."

With this analysis of the corruption that comes from love of earthly money in contrast with earthly contentment combined with thanksgiving for grace, we can see Jesus' parable of the rich man and Lazarus in a new light. Surely the reference to the need for the rich man's brothers to repent suggests that he was not only rich by circumstance but was trapped by the intentionality of lust for the sumptuous lifestyle and was not generous to the poor man at his gate. Similarly Lazarus was not only poor but thankful for even that. What is striking about Jesus' parable is its finality: It's too late to repent in Hades, and the brothers don't get more than the prophets for warning.

Neither Paul nor I want to trivialize the finality of life by associating it with paying tuition, taking out student loans, and other instruments for living out our commitment. But the truth is that commitment is lived out in small things like these. The choice before us is fake life or the life that is truly life. Fake life is like the love of money that leads into all kinds of evils, temptations, and enslavements. True life regards our personal circumstances with contentment, focuses on the ministry of holiness and justice, and finds its plumb line and balance in being able constantly to give thanks to God for the grace that is true wealth. The commitment to true life is made in constant and repeated choices in small things. There is no end to God's mercy and help, and thus nothing final in this sense. But in the end we either have chosen the true life of crucifixion plus the resurrection with early rain and the outpouring of Spirit, or we have not. Like the rich man, we have the prophets, and also Christ, the apostles, and our own ministry of conveying the healing word of true life. With all that grace the choice is still ours. "Today I set before you the choice between life and death; choose life!" (from Deuteronomy 30:15-20). The way to be rich after paying tuition is to choose all the parts of the life of thanksgiving to God for true wealth. Here is a path home to life. Welcome.

This was the fall 1992 matriculation sermon, preached in Marsh Chapel on September 27.

29. Editing and Embellishing the News

Read and reflect on Exodus 20:1-4, 7-9, 12-20; Psalm 19;
Philippians 3:4b-14; Matthew 21:33-46.

The title of this sermon, "Editing and Embellishing the News," bespeaks a seminary function about which we have some ambivalence and keep silence before bishops. *Of course* we edit out some representations of the gospel that previous generations thought important. *Of course* we embellish what we have inherited to address new occasions and the duties they bring. We try with all the many disciplines we can muster to edit and embellish responsibly. Academics aside, the strongest ecclesiastical argument for intellectual rigor and demanding disciplined creativity for the careful examination and critical review of our work, which requires faculty publication and professional life, derives from the need to edit and embellish the gospel responsibly. And the strongest argument against theological fashion and fads, against responsiveness to the self-proclaimed agenda of the needy, against politically correct ideologies and movement politics is that all those things powerfully undermine the attempt to edit and embellish responsibly. Jesus never conformed to pressures of the vanguard or rearguard, and he never asked, "What can I do for you?" He was the paradigm editor and embellisher in our religion.

But he was neither the first nor last. The editors of the Revised Common Lectionary have taken the extremely daring step of editing the Ten Commandments. (Your sheet indicates the passages left out.) The previous Common Lectionary (unrevised) appointed the whole of the Ten Commandments, Exodus 20:1-20. I asked Boston University professor Horace Allen, a member of the editorial committee for the revision, what the motive was. His notes indicate only that they wanted to shorten the passage. So we can ask what unstated principles are at work when the changes are for brevity.

Verses 5-6 are not hard to figure out. First, they depict God in an extremely anthropomorphic way; so do verses 10 and 11. As such they are in cognitive dissonance with verse 4 condemning idolatry: Verbal idolatry is surely as bad as sculptural. Second, to say God is jealous is to get in trouble with people who believe that theodicy requires God always to be morally uplifting; jealousy is a green-eyed monster. I suspect myself that the jealousy theme here has less to do with emotions than with securing the ties of the covenant with Israel, which is the overall theme of the larger passage of which the Ten Commandments is a part. Third, verses 5 and 6 depict God as neglecting moral responsibility in favor of moral consequences, by visiting the sins of the parents to generations of children. That point had already been edited, long before Jesus, by Ezekiel who asserted the priority of personal responsibility over moral consequences. He wrote, in the eighteenth chapter of his prophecy at verse 20, "A child shall not suffer for the iniquity of a parent, nor a parent suffer for the iniquity of a child; the righteousness of the righteous shall be his own, and the wickedness of the wicked shall be his own." Ezekiel and the subsequent tradition, of course, were thinking not about consequences in this life but rather about effects of actions on moral standing as judged by God. Knowing ourselves that sometimes the good suffer greatly and the wicked prosper like the green bay tree, we agree with the editors that moral standing is more important than the consequences of moral or immoral acts. Aristotle, I might note however, agreed with Moses: You cannot tell whether people are happy, he said, until they know whether their grandchildren are happy on whom their own happiness in large part depends. We who struggle with the spiritual and material welfare of inner cities know that much is to be said for moral consequences: Evil lasts for generations and poisons babies before they are born; holy parents are made wretched by wicked children. I suppose God should not be held responsible for this, but this is God's world. The editors are taking sides in a complex issue.

The editorial omission of verses 10-11, as I mentioned, removes excessive anthropomorphism. It also eliminates the tacit approval of slavery and the assumption that you ought to be able to control your children and guests. The more subtle editorial point is that, although the remaining text says to work only six days and remember the seventh as holy, the editing eliminates the point that God worked only six days and consecrated the seventh *because* he rested. That point repeats the Genesis account of creation but it still stands in strong cognitive dissonance with the main point of Genesis, which is that the work of the first six days was good. Sabbath rest is *not better* than creative work for God or Israel, according to the editors. What subtle shifts of emphasis are involved in editing! How often there are two sides, and one or both has support from a political agenda.

Our schools need to be particularly conscious of the forces that bias our editing of the tradition and interpretation of the current situation. Most of us were educated in the days when Neo-Orthodoxy said that the gospel is like a thrown stone to be picked up or left, that the distinction between who is inside and who outside the Christian movement is more important than any other, that the writings of Paul are vastly superior to the Gospels, and that those who question the Neo-Orthodox edition of Christianity are not mistaken for reasons that can be examined, but are simply illegitimate, not Christians, mere philosophers. In our own time as seminary leaders, many in the civil rights, feminist, and liberation movements have argued from the true premise that the voices of the oppressed ought to be heard to the false conclusion that their agenda, itself the product of oppression, is by itself the compelling edition of the gospel. We all struggle to balance the competing claims of the privileged oppressed for whom no advantages are enough.

Jesus' parable of the absentee vintner shows how confusing this is. As with other parables the dicey question is who we, the hearers, are supposed to be. It seems, of course, that the wicked tenants are to be identified with the crowd Jesus was addressing, filled mainly with righteous religious people who were, Jesus was predicting, about to lose the kingdom. But then insofar as we and our students hear this parable, we like to think of ourselves as the slaves and perhaps even the son of the owner, going into the world to demand justice and demand for God the divine rent. At least we hope to train our students to call the world to account and not to be surprised at the ambiguous welcome they might receive. How poignant it is that the son has to be taken out of the vineyard, out of his father's property, into merely alien land in order to be killed. That's even worse than a dean or president being called to the Trustees' office. As for my own institution, we have such a strong and unbridled love of social justice that I suspect some faculty and students would identify not with the tenants nor the emissaries but with the executioners come to remove the tenants. Note that it was not Jesus but the crowd in response that brought up the point about putting the wicked tenants to death. Oh, how we love justice when it is them, not us! How we edit the tradition depends in large measure on discovering our own true identity in the parables.

In our seminaries the crucial question is who we and our students are. The students tend to answer that question in terms of the place from which they've come. At a recent meeting of a group to design accrediting standards for the Association of Theological Schools, the point was made that the one common trait of the students at Catholic, fundamentalist, and mainline Protestant seminaries is that they all come from dysfunctional families. I demurred for Boston University, claiming that we have more than a dozen happy and healthy students for whom we are planning a support group to help them fit in.

By contrast to the students' self-identification, we and the faculty pray the students can be identified by their future service, by their mission, by their readiness to be ministers in a corrupt and oppressing world, by their functional membership in the effective body of Christ. But past identity is more comfortable than a future defined by challenge; the struggle to shift our students' identifying orientation is difficult indeed.

For help here we can look to Paul's point in Philippians where he moves straight from editing to embellishment. Paul's past was by no means dysfunctional. He was raised by and perfected in the practice of the latest Pharisaic edition of Judaism. Jesus himself was part of this Pharisaic movement to transform Judaism. Unlike those of our students who glory in the stigmata of dysfunctionalism, Paul gave up even the best in his inherited identity to take on the new life of Christ. First he took on the resurrection of Christ and then he took on the sufferings. New life in Christ, participating first in his resurrection, gives us the strength to deepen identity with him and to go through suffering and death with him also.

Paul's writings themselves are in need of a bit of editing. To call serious religious training "rubbish" presents a grave danger to the alumnae/i fund; the lectionary committee should have caught that. But Paul's main point gives the principle for our embellishment of the gospel that is as inevitable for us as editing. Macedonian Philippi was a different world from Palestinian Galilee. Paul had to embellish the thought-world of Jesus and his first disciples with the extraordinarily more cosmopolitan culture of Hellenism. How did he do that? By wit and scholarship, of course. But he does not even mention that here. He embellished the gospel by bringing the Philippians in to participate as a congregation in the ongoing ministry of Jesus.

193

The crucial point is that Jesus' ministry is ongoing. Paul could not attempt to repeat Jesus' rural Galilean ministry of even one short generation before in urban Hellenized Philippi. We, like Paul, enter Jesus' ministry as it goes on far from the earthly life of Jesus. We get our bearings, of course, from understanding how Jesus' ministry has grown with edited and embellished changes from ancient Galilee to us in Chicago. We tremble at the heroic models of saints like Paul and Wesley who gave that ministry decisive new forms and directions, knowing we are called to equally heroic tasks. We tremble in a different sense at the terrible examples of false saints like the King Louis IX and the Christian Nazis who wretchedly misdirected Christ's ministry and pray we shall be kept from that.

To enter into Christ's ministry in our own time and place, as we do when we train students for it, is truly to participate in the life of Jesus, beginning with resurrection and digging in through suffering and death. Without responsible editing to engage the tradition of the church's ministry beginning with Jesus, we fail to define ourselves with Christ's divine identity. But without responsible embellishment of that ministry to address the issues of our time, to hear and answer the voices of our needy, to participate in the sufferings of our age, we fail to make Christ's identity incarnate here. If we are to participate in the death and resurrection of God incarnate, we must define ourselves by the ministry of Jesus but also, like Paul, have the faith to give up all secure accomplishments to embody Christ's life anew. Jesus lives in our time only if we have that faith.

Let us therefore approach the communion table conscious of the need to balance engaged memorial and committed risk. On the one hand the elements recollect Jesus' broken body and spilt blood by which we remember the path to glory. As we repeat the supper again and again, shaping our expectations by this death and resurrection figure, we take on ever more intimately the particular person of Jesus carried to us by others who have accepted the bread and drunk the cup.

On the other hand, the elements symbolize nourishment for the tasks at hand. The levels of meaning of nourishment are many and all-powerful. This is the table fellowship through which Jesus taught and inspired his disciples to extend his ministry. At the deep, largely unconscious level this is the cannibal feast by which we take on Jesus' powers and virtues through eating him. With this meal we can let go of our past dysfunctions and accomplishments and, with Paul, move on to what the life of Christ requires today.

None of this tells us exactly how to edit so as to engage Christ and the tradition truly, nor how to embellish the inherited practices of ministry so as to be the New Being of Christ in all the places of our time. These issues of judgment constitute the essence of the labor in the seminary vineyards. They are what we are about. Let us come to the table with prayer for responsibility in editing and embellishing so that we and our fellow disciples might remember who we are becoming and take nourishment for the tasks that require us to move our feet surely across the earth while our eyes are fixed on glory. Amen.

The Association of United Methodist Theological Schools brings together the presidents of the free standing United Methodist seminaries and the deans of the university-based theological schools twice a year. Most of the time is spent in discussion of the vast array of problems and opportunities for theological education in our time, from how to pay for seminary without bankrupting our students with loans to how to respond to the call for theological education in eastern Europe. But part of each fall meeting is a retreat with spouses in which we come together as a support group, especially in regard to worship and family life. On October 3, 1993, I preached this sermon for our worship, conducted by Beth Neville, which was held in the chapel at Garrett-Evangelical Theological School in Evanston, Illinois, under the sponsorship of President Neal Fisher and Reverend Ila Fisher. We included in the service bulletin the lectionary version of the Ten Commandments.

30. PROBLEMS TO SOLVE IN SEMINARY

Read and reflect on Job 1:1, 2:1-10; Hebrews 1:1-4, 2:5-12;
Mark 10:2-16.

Permit me to reinforce the welcomes already expressed to new students in the Division and School of Theology and add to them a word of comfort. Some of you now might be doubting the wisdom of your decision to matriculate here. Boston is more expensive than you had planned. The course syllabi you have received demand an unanticipated quantity of work that marks the serious difference between undergraduate and graduate school. Our community is not as perfectly supportive as you had hoped. And although everyone is friendly and more than willing to give you directions about where to go and what to do, few know whereof they speak. As Paul said in 3 Timothy 3:42, "Longing for heaven, you may think you have arrived when in fact it is only South Thessaloniki." Nevertheless, there are overwhelmingly persuasive reasons why you were right to come to the seminary and to the Division to study religion, and those reasons are laid out in the scriptures you have heard read.

The texts for today's service are those assigned for next Sunday in the Revised Common Lectionary. But either because of divine providence, which would be Calvin's hypothesis, or because of Horace Allen's scheming influence on the committee that drew up the lectionary, which is my hypothesis, the selection of texts is particularly apt for matriculation day. For the texts together raise most of the major problems of religion for our time, and they present what most of us would have thought are the wrong answers. Consider them in turn.

The passage from Job opens with "heavenly beings" presenting themselves to God. The phrase translated "heavenly beings" in Hebrew really means "sons of God." The New Revised Standard Version of the Bible translates it "heavenly beings" in respect of its policy of avoiding gender-exclusive language wherever possible. I agree with that policy because the use of scripture in worship and devotional life demands that scripture be assessed as a present reality, not merely as a trace of an ancient reality. But you also need continually to bear in mind that what we now call "heavenly beings" were called "sons of God" by the biblical writers and that the present reality of the scripture is a fixed-up version. Part of what is lost in this fix-up is the connection with the New Testament ascription of the common name, Son of God, to Jesus. To be alive in the present is to be translating the past to the future, with all the ambiguities of gain and loss that involves. Never again, after this place, can you take an English translation of the Bible for only what it says. Christian ministry began at Pentecost with a burst of translations and continues to be that always, with ambiguous results. But be glad you've come here to learn how to be faithful and true while fixing up your translations, the first of the reasons I mentioned.

Another point to notice in Job is that the word "Satan," which has become for us a proper name for the devil, in that text merely means "accuser," the description of an active and legitimate role in the heavenly court. What that role supposes is that we live under judgment. To be human is to be under obligation to God and to creation. The human condition is to have obligations and to be judged for them. This basic point is presupposed throughout the Bible and is made in various ways by nearly every religion on earth. But fundamental obligation and judgment seem to run wholly counter to the modern point of view in which people are understood primarily within the frameworks of psychological and sociological causation. Emphasis on the divine grounding of obligation and judgment is believed to foster crippling guilt feelings and to represent God as punitive Father-figure. We prefer to think of the wicked as victims determined by forces beyond their control, particularly when the wicked in question are ourselves. But the point of religion is to call us to personal and communal responsibility for our obligations to God and to the divine grounding of our obligations to other people and nature. You were right to come to study religion to find out how to be responsible and modern at once.

The most offensive point of the Job text, of course, is its clear treatment of God as the author of suffering. In our passage, God commissions the accuser to apply tortures; and Job himself remarks, without doubting, that his suffering comes from God. Our current religious wisdom, to the contrary, is that God is supposed to be good and cannot be the author of suffering or evil. You yourselves have asked many times, have you not, how God could allow the bloodletting in Bosnia and Rwanda, the ravages of AIDS and Alzheimer's, or your own personal pains and tragedies? Many contemporary theologians have argued that God has to be conceived as finite so that the sources of suffering and evil can be conceived as forces God cannot sufficiently control. Many of our contemporaries like to think of God not as creator but as cocreator, requiring our cooperation and suffering when we do not give it. But these modern views of God are far too domesticated for Job. Job's God, you know, leaps to take responsibility for everything; and when Job calls God to account for sending undeserved pain, God answers from the whirlwind that the human kind of responsibility has no relevance for the creator who lays the foundations of the earth. It's good you've come here to learn how God is bigger, fiercer, more untamed, and wilder than the domesticated gods urged upon us by those who hope divinity is safe for moral negotiation.

One last point before leaving Job: When Job notes that suffering comes from God, he blesses God for it. "Shall we receive the good at the hand of God and not the bad?" A passage close to our text says, "The Lord gave, and the Lord has taken away, blessed be the name of the Lord." How can we bless God for the pain and evil in our lives? I had cited that passage with approval in a book that was in the copyediting stage of production when our daughter died. Deciding subsequently whether to leave the citation in was the hardest theology I had done to date. If Job is right, then liberation theologies have a more limited sphere of application than they are wont to claim. Or perhaps Job is wrong and it is better to curse God or find God a scapegoat. Fortunately, M.Div. students have three years to figure this out. Although M.T.S. students will have to work a little faster, doctoral students have the leisure to get it right. It is a good thing you are here to work on the problem.

The text from Hebrews is a deeply intriguing reworking of Jewish symbols into Christian form. It opens by identifying Jesus with one of those "Sons of God," and contrasting that status of sonship with the status of angels. Angels are identified in chapter 1:7 with winds and flames of fire, that is, with the symbols of the Holy Spirit. Jesus as Son of God is above angels, and moreover can raise us above them as true heirs, brothers and sisters. I hope you develop the ear to catch the echoes of these developing symbols: Hebrew Bible angels coalesce to become the New Testament

Holy Spirit; Hebrew Bible Sons of God attain singleness in the Christ. You will never worship freely nor understand those who do without hearing these symbols play, interweave, reverse, and produce overtones sounded by no one symbol alone. How right you were to come here to learn how today's symbols have deep and different echoes, and that when these echoes are damped, the symbols die to become doctrines.

But the punch in the Hebrews text is the interpretation of Christ's suffering as saving sacrifice. The Levitical rites for purifying sinners and other unclean beings become the atonement rite of purification of all sins. Jesus' death is the sacrifice no priest can make save God alone. Yet how can we believe this? Can we believe that the suffering of the innocent can redeem the guilty? Feminists sometimes claim that is the rationalization used to abuse women. Liberals say all suffering is bad and that Jesus suffered because he was courageous and unlucky. Conservatives treat atonement as a pawnshop transaction having to do with human merit. How can we take it to heart that sin is closer to blasphemy and dirt than to injustice and alienation? How can our hope be fixed on the washing redemption of innocent purity rather than some magic that fixes our brokenness? Hebrews says that God receives us into the family in which we shall be washed and shine with divine glory. If that baptism in the blood of the sacrifice is enough to provoke us onto the path of sanctification, to pursue righteousness, piety, faith, and hope for amending the world and our lives, the responsibility for sanctification is ours. If you do not understand that, or understand it and do not like it, be glad you are here to find out what is at stake. These texts confront us with the ideas and vocabulary that have estranged Christianity from the European enlightenment. We are heirs of both, and one or the other is an embarrassment.

From the sublimity of Hebrews' high symbols and dogmas, Mark's text takes us to the sweaty issues of sexual ethics, Jesus' rejection of divorce. Most everyone nowadays, including myself, believes that divorce is allowable, even desirable, under a variety of circumstances. Jesus' rigorism seems cruel. I have two glosses on this text, both about things Jesus did not say. First, whereas Jesus was quite clear on divorce, he said nothing about homosexuality; so those who take a rejecting view of homosexuality need to be even more outspoken in condemning divorce if they are to claim a biblical warrant. Second, Jesus cited the only passage from Scripture I know to say that the man leaves his family to unite with the wife to become one flesh; most representations of marriage in the Hebrew Bible are clear that the wife leaves her family to join the husband and his family. The

Genesis 2:24 passage Jesus cited makes no mention of family except for leaving it, and no mention of children. Sex is not necessarily for procreation although that is sometimes the result. For Jesus, marriage was the forming of husband and wife into one flesh with no mention of anyone else. You can see why, within this imagery, divorce is a butchering of a two-person/one-flesh organism. You can see why also Jesus took human relations to be more important than roles and circumstances. We have trouble taking sex as seriously as Jesus did. Those versions of Christianity who turn Jesus' remark into a matter of law miss that point entirely. There are no quick answers to these questions of sexual ethics. If you serve a church, you will be torn many ways and will be called upon to advise and bless where you would rather duck and curse. Be glad you have some time here to uncover the snares.

Gender issues, tradition and authority, the transformations of symbols, ultimate obligations, divine judgment, suffering and evil, God's goodness and responsibility, blessing all life or only its good parts, the identity of Jesus, sin and atonement, sexual ethics—if you dealt with no more than these issues in Christianity or any religion, your plate of religious studies would be full. None of these issues is resolved between scripture and liberal sensibilities. Alas, this list is abbreviated and superficial. You are people to whom others will turn for answers. Now is your time to find out what to say before you are responsible for souls in these matters. Many of you have been called to be responsible for souls, and those of you who want only to teach will be responsible, called or not. As your faculty is.

Permit me two brief theological reflections. The fact that each of the positions represented by the biblical authors in our texts goes contrary to our current largely common sympathies adds to the following cumulative theological position that this world is God's, not ours. The popular opposition or uneasiness I have mentioned in each case with reference to the scripture's assertions comes from our attempts to bank the divine fires to a human measure. Proud as we are to suppose that the human moral and creative project is the measure of all things, in reality that is illusion, according to scripture. Those humane things are noble and to be pursued with all our effort—they are our tasks—but in the long run they are vanity; and with respect to them the truth is the cross, the bare unearthly measure of human goodwill and striving. The Bible says this is God's world, which is flushed with a glory strangely indifferent to our scale.

The second point, which can only be understood after the first, is the good news every sermon is obliged to announce. When Job sought like a fool to indict a God whose standing transcends all moral measure, God came in a whirlwind to tell him about it. Friends, even deans see the glory in the clouds of witnesses and the pillars of support for your education and ministry. You will not answer all the questions you find here, and you will believe your heart, mind, soul, and strength always to fall short, which will be true. Our striving will be vain even though it is our calling. But, friends, bright glory's mirror shows that in God we have been purified like children at the knee of Jesus; and for that reason—not for salvation, not for goodness, not for wholeness, health, nor ministry—we shall run the good race set before us, course by course, test by test, to understand what we ought to know and thereby to better do the work that is our lot. Welcome. To God be the glory. Amen.

This is the sermon preached for matriculation in fall 1994, preached in Marsh Chapel on September 27.

31. Prophets in Deep Water

Read and reflect on Isaiah 6:1-13, Psalm 138, 1 Corinthians 15:1-11, Luke 5:1-11.

This service of matriculation serves to celebrate the new people who have joined our scholarly community and also to remind the rest of us, as Paul wanted to remind the Corinthians, of what we already know but tend to neglect. In our case that fragile knowledge is that the scholarly community needs constant nurture because new people are always arising within it, and veterans departing. As Paul wrote to Timothy in his third letter to him (at 6:73), "Just as a pharaoh who knew not Joseph caused untold trouble, so new students need to be told what you take for granted everyone knows. That they feel called to the gospel does not mean they know that to which they are called, or who called them, or why." The Boston University School of Theology has sometimes been called the "School of Prophets." Our texts today are about prophecy and calling, and they serve to recall our attention to why we are here.

There are four texts, you will have noted: Psalm 138, as well as Isaiah 6, 1 Corinthians 15, and Luke 5. Professor Allen, the expert in the lectionary by which they are assigned for today, can tell you why he and his conspirators put these together, and I suggest you ask him until he can give a plausible answer. Meanwhile, I would like to provide a preacher's orientation by reviewing some of the common and dissimilar elements.

All four texts have to do with calling, but disagree about who calls and who is called. The psalm cites the psalmist as calling upon God to get him (or her) out of trouble. By contrast the other three cite God as calling upon some person. In Isaiah the phantasmagoric image of God enthroned and supplied with winged courtiers calls on Isaiah, the man of unclean lips, to go prophesy for God. In Luke, Jesus calls Peter and the other fishermen to go fishing for people. In 1 Corinthians, Paul tells how he was called, as one untimely born, to be an apostle; and we know from other passages that this was done in a visionary experience of the risen Christ.

The four texts differ widely in the imagery of calling. The psalm is in the form of a song of thanksgiving. Isaiah uses the image of fire, a burning coal that purifies the lips. Luke uses the image of deep water and fishing for the drowning, an image that resonates with baptism themes. Paul's calling, as described in Acts 9, took the form of blinding light and the spoken words of Jesus. Thanksgiving, fire, water, light, and the Word are major biblical themes, but not particularly coherent with one another nor necessarily associated with calling.

With regard to the purpose of calling, the psalmist simply wants help. Isaiah relates an unexpected purpose, namely that the prophet should speak in such a way that the people will *not* understand, so that they will *not* be healed but continue their evil until the land is devastated and they are scattered in exile. In one sense, we must suppose, this is Isaiah attempting to put a religious interpretation on a destruction and exile that have already taken place. But for the interpretation to be successful, he has to intend the religious meaning involved, namely, that sometimes things cannot get better until they get worse; or to put it another way, people who are forgiven little are thankful only a little and love little more than they have to. Luke represents Jesus as calling disciples to join in his ministry, which in the occasion at hand, is to minister to the crowd of people pressing in on Jesus "to hear the Word of God." Paul is called to extend that ministry far away and to arrange its being passed to the next generation; but in the case of the Corinthians his calling is to strengthen a faith previously planted, to give it focus and institutional staying power. To get help, to give 'em hell, to nourish people with the Word of God, and to guide people through the ongoing Christian life are the four callings of our texts.

Diverse as these texts are, there is an underlying common theme more basic than any I have mentioned, namely, that in all the calling and sending, it is God's purpose that is to be fulfilled. Even the psalm, which seems to be all about the psalmist's purpose, ends this way:

> The Lord will fulfill his purpose for me;
> > your steadfast love, O LORD, endures forever.
> Do not forsake the work of your hands. (v. 8)

203

The point is that God is at work, in helping the psalmist, in sending Isaiah, in calling disciples for Jesus, fellow fishers, and in making Paul an apostle. Most of us have come to this institution because we want God to work through us and we need to be prepared. But before we become too confident that God has a work for us, and that we have identified what that is, let me ask with whom we identify in the four texts.

Those of us intending to become pastors, or who already are pastors, most obviously identify with Paul in trying to keep his congregation focused. In fact, the whole of 1 Corinthians is a kind of manual on how to deal with common problems in congregational life. Paul talks about coping with factional bickering, with loyalty to different ministers, with how to conduct worship so as not to set the rich against the poor, how to deal with other religions—especially when represented in the families of Christians and when practical matters of diet are involved—and with how to distinguish and appropriately honor the many kinds of ministry involved in the Christian life, both within the congregation and in the congregation's mission to the larger community. Our text for today comes immediately after an extended discussion of diverse ministries and how you should not let anyone hog all the time or set the tone in church meetings. The point of our text is to recall the Corinthians from this plurality back to their basic point of origin, their original gospel. Paul, you heard, runs through a first draft of the creed, stating that Jesus died for our sins, that he rose from the dead and appeared to successively wider groups of disciples, thereby launching the Christian movement that now includes the Corinthians and the Bostonians. I rather like Paul's draft of the creed because it emphasizes the step by step passing down of the saving power of Jesus, a succession of callings. By the time the committee got through with the creed in the third and fourth centuries, that point was reduced to a mention of the catholic church and the communion of saints. Pastors identify with Paul in this text because we too cope with these problems.

On the other hand, perhaps we should identify more with the Corinthians. Don't we bicker in the pride of our righteousness? What one of us utters as prophecy another hears as abusive speech. Some of us want to worship a certain way, and others find that boring or offensive. Some of us think ministry is one thing; others think it is another and not the first. And don't we all sometimes lose focus on why we are here when distracted by the diversities of ministries to be learned? Because the basics of the faith are so hard to understand in the twentieth century, so hard to express in ways that move the heart as they ought, we are tempted to divert ourselves into assorted ministries to others and private devotional speeches in tongues. We need to be recalled to what brings us to God in the first place, and thus we are in the place of the Corinthians who need a letter from Paul.

In Luke's story, we professional Christians easily identify with the disciples being called to be fishers of people. Most of us understand our lives to be a late extension of the ministry of Jesus. For many, the calling was like being told to move out into deep water and having one's expectations reversed. Many have given up very much, if not everything, to follow Jesus in ministry.

But before we get too professional about this, I suggest that we might identify instead with the crowd of people who were pressing around Jesus so hard as to push him into the water. He had to borrow a boat to set up a preaching station. Luke says "the crowd was pressing in upon him to hear the word of God." Who needs to hear the Word of God more than those who profess to preach it? Peter left his boat to follow Jesus only after he had been with him in the boat when Jesus preached. If we are honest, the deeper part of our soul is not the fisher, the preacher, the servant minister, but the thirsty seeker wanting the Word; for it is in the Word that we live and move and have our being. We need nothing else and secretly yearn for it more than for riches, power, or even purpose. Unless we are first in the crowd pressing in on Jesus, we have no business responding to any call to ministry.

Now in the case of Isaiah there is very good reason not to identify with the people to whom the prophet is sent, for they are stiff-necked and uncomprehending. They go from bad to worse, and the Lord seems to be behind their ruin. Far better to be with the prophet, to be abased by God's glory, seared by the purifying coals, and sent to an undeserving and hostile people. Many times in ministry accumulated frustrations will make it seem as if we had Isaiah's mission to a people who only get worse. Why, we ask, do our best efforts, hard won by our own purifying struggles and repeated humiliations, only bring out the worst in people? Our divinely ordained purpose seems to be a lost cause, and we keep going only because the commission seemed to be so powerful and lifted up.

Of course this way of identifying with Isaiah, with its grandiosity and self-pity, reveals our true identification with the perverse people to whom Isaiah was sent. If we complain that we are suffering for the gospel, lament that our efforts are unrecognized, pout when people are unresponsive, grumble about the disciplines of study, gripe that teachers are unfair, whine that life is too stressful, then things have not yet gotten bad enough for us to abandon ourselves to God. If we follow the god of our own religious success, we will have to be pushed to disaster to see that this is not the true God. What fear and trembling do we have before the God whose purification is not a quick hot touch to the lips but a course of ruin, disaster, homelessness, and misery? You see how we identify with the psalmist: Help us, Lord, against our enemies, who most hurtfully are ourselves. Thank you, Lord, for sparing us from ruin. Be fulfilled in us, whatever that requires.

In the long run, of course, it does not matter with whom we identify. What matters is the identity God gives us. The real actor in all our texts, the real cause, the real grantor of identity is God, and God-given identity is shocking. The one point I would like you to take with you from these texts when you head out into deep water is how shocking the whole business is. Paul was blinded, struck dumb, and turned around forever. Peter and his partners saw through Jesus' miraculous overwhelming of their boat with fish to the Holy One of Israel fishing them out of ordinary life into Kingdom life. Isaiah saw the Lord high and lifted up, more dazzling than the healing serpent lifted in the wilderness, more obvious than the Christ lifted up to sway the world. He saw himself at last in truth, a priest in the temple sanctum, unclean, unclean, expelled from ordinary service to carry God's destiny from temple to the world. Shocking, uncanny, hardly to be believed.

Now I ask you to look for the shock of God in our lives. Most of the time we struggle to comprehend the unfamiliar in the familiar. We clothe God in the image of a supervising parent or a master sergeant giving us our mission. We translate the call of God to a career for which we can prepare and whose course we can scope. But for a moment I want us to comprehend in the other direction. Let us set aside our anthropomorphic images of God giving us directions and abandon ourselves to the wild God sung by seraphs and strange things, the God of fire and water and light, the God who wastes generations and saves all, the God who judges us into abject humility and amends our hearts in perfect love, the God in glory high and lifted up who draws us to that glory by a plain path that unfolds day by day. Jesus loves us, what a shock!

In face of that mystery let us set aside the controlled images of our career and abandon ourselves to the strange work God has for us, to the good news that looks like bad news, to the projects that we will not finish, to the lost causes that end in glory, to the journeys far from home, to the tasks we cannot comprehend, to the people whose love we do not deserve, to the future that is not ours but God's. For the paradox of the faith is that only when we leave the familiar and launch out into deep water can we delight in the love of God that lights up the ordinary and makes God's work of our humble work. In no other way does it make sense that people as timid, self-pitying, arrogant, unskilled, slow-witted, tired, and self-destructive as ourselves, beset by enemies, hell-bent on destruction, incompetent at church life, and parched by thirst for the Word should be identified by God with the work of salvation. What a shock that God loves the world to glory, and that we are that loving, every broken one of us rising through to glory.

Our schooltime thoughts will quickly turn from these mysteries of the faith to courses, assignments, and lunch. The diversity and scatteredness of our lives are part of finite living. But it is important to be reminded, from time to time, of what we already know and the newcomers begin to appreciate, that it is God who is in this place, God who has heard us calling, God who has called us, and God who sends us forth, prophets. Amen.

This was the matriculation sermon preached for spring 1995 on January 31 in Marsh Chapel.